INGVAR

GUID

SVALBARD

THE ARCTIC PEARL

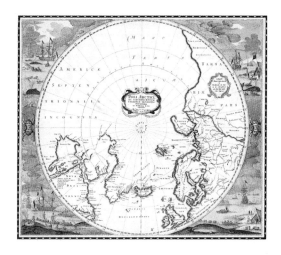

Contents

Getting to Svalbard

At Tromsø airport I pass through "The Gate to the Arctic" to wait for the airplane that will take me to Svalbard. So many thoughts and questions come to me as I pass through the gate. What will I experience? Will I see polar bears? How do people survive in this area so close to the North Pole? Will there be drift ice? How big are the glaciers? Will I be able to reach the place where Andrée started his balloon flight to the North Pole?
Yes, there are so many thoughts and questions in my mind. I am ful of expectations and I sit down on a sofa and study a brochure on Svalbard. There is some text on the different

parts of the islands, above all on Spitsbergen, which is the biggest island. It is the west coast of this island that is inhabited by people, and there are three communities, two Norwegian and one Russian. In the middle of the west coast of the island there is Isfjorden, a spectacular fjord, and there you find Barentsburg, the Russian community. Further into the fjord there is Longyearbyen, the large Norwegian community. At Kongsfjorden further north you find the other Norwegian community, Ny-Ålesund.

At last is the boarding call for the plane to Svalbard. There are quite many of us who are travelling and we are a mixed group. Some of us seem to be travelling in the line of work, but judging by their clothes there are also those among us who are going on an adventure in the Arctic Wilderness.

The plane takes off, and I find that northern Norway is very beautiful. There are mountains, many islands and a shifting landscape of fields, lakes and forests. We leave the Norwegian mainland and fly over the Arctic Ocean. After approximately an hour we pass Bjørnøya, which is a part of Svalbard even though it is situated right in between Norway and Svalbard. A little later the southern part of Spitsbergen appears, and we fly in over a landscape where clouds lie thick. The highest mountain peaks stick up like bluish-black spears. Then the clouds drift away and soon all Spitsbergen is in front of us, sun-drenched. A fantastic view. I see mountains and valleys, glaciers and fjords. The plane turns to the north before landing at the airport of Longyearbyen, and we pass Ny-Ålesund, which is 110 to 120 kilometres north of Longyearbyen. The mountains here are rather flat on top, and I see clearly how they have been cut by the movements of the glaciers. 60% of the area of Svalbard is covered by glaciers, and I do believe that is true when I see all these masses of ice.

The sound of the engines intensifies, and we slowly descend towards the landing strip. The wheels touch the concrete, and for the first time I am on Svalbard ground. When I leave the aircraft I notice that the air is cooler than in Tromsø. A thermometre shows me we have plus 10° C.
The sun is shining, and there is a light, western breeze along the fjord. I enter the air terminal to pick up my luggage in the crowded hall. Everybody is pushing and shoving to find their suitcases, backpackages, diving equipment or whatever they bring along.
When at last I have found my luggage, I walk to the bus, that will take me to the centre of Longyearbyen. When there I step out and take a good look around full of expectation. The buildings are much more modern than I had imagined. The mountains dominate the view, several hundred metres high, and I can look out over the Adventfjorden, on which the community is situated.

Facts for Visitors

The simplest and most common way of getting to Svalbard is by air from Tromsø. One can go there by boat too, but only during the summer. Some travel agencies arrange trips to Svalbard and offer package tours including a round trip combined with certain tours for instance along the west coast of Spitsbergen. It is also possible to take a flight to Longyearbyen and buy different excursions from the local operators. They offer boat trips around the entire Svalbard or along parts of the west coast. A helicopter can take you to Ny-Ålesund and other places on the islands, but this is quite expensive.

Excursions

Excursions ranging from one to several days can be arranged. You can for example buy a ski trip or a snowmobile-tour, guides included. You can visit a coal mine, go fossil hunting, join a flower-walk, take a trip in a kayak etc. Prices range from some hundred Norwegian crowns to several thousand crowns.

The Norwegian authorities advice tourists to use tour operators that provide trips with an armed guide. If you are familiar with firearms and decide to arrange excursions on your own you can rent rifles in Longyearbyen.You must have a weapon to be able to defend yourself against polar bears.

Registration

In an area around Longyearbyen, Sveagruva and Barentsburg you are allowed to go on tours without having to register at Sysselmannen´s office, the Governor´s office. This is also possible around Ny-Ålesund. However *it is advisable to register all tours* in these areas, particularly if you are going on a longer tour. Registration means that you hand in your itinerary so that the authorities know where to send a rescue team if needed. A visitor who plans his own tours will also have to guarantee that there are sufficient funds available in case of rescue – either through an insurance or by having funds in a bank account.

Clothing and Other Equipment

It is important that you have the clothes needed depending on the season and on the excursions and tours you want to take part in. In summer the appropriate clothing is what you wear in autumn in the Alps. In winter very warm clothes are needed.

IMPORTANT!

It is better to be too warmly dressed and be able to peel off clothes – than to have too thin or the wrong clothing and get wet and cold. Several layers of t-shirts and sweaters are by far better than wearing one shirt and a thick sweater. Principle-of-many-layers!

Recommended clothing for cruise-ship tours

On boat it is possible to have ordinary clothes for indoor use but on deck you need warm, windproof clothes, rainclothes, a windproof cap, gloves and ordinary winter shoes. It can be both cold and windy and even rainy when you want to admire the beautiful sceneries or the polar bear, who might appear. While disembarking in a rubber dinghy warm clothes are a must – and so are rainclothes (you may go soaked when travelling in the rubber boat). You will also need boots or hiking boots. When walking in the terrain ordinary shoes are simply not good enough.

If you travel in one of the big cruise-ships you will be expected to change for dinner, something that is customary in these circumstances.

Suggested clothing for day-tours during summer

You should have boots or hiking boots depending on what tour you take part in. In the wilderness normal shoes are not of any use at all. Warm, windproof clothes, rainwear, cap and gloves are suitable clothes but of course the weather and the character of the tour will influence your choice of clothing.

Suggested clothing for tours lasting more than one day in summer

First and foremost you will need boots or hiking boots and for the rest warm, windproof clothes, rainwear, a windproof cap and windproof gloves. Then you will also need a change of trousers, several pairs of warm hiking socks, warm ordinary socks, warm underwear such as long johns, t-shirts, shirts, sweaters and light rubber shoes plus a sewing kit. A backpack of at least 75 litres will be needed to store all equipment. You will also need a

The ice front at Brepollen, Hornsund

waterproof cover for the backpack and plastic bags to protect your equipment from getting wet.

To spend the night in the wilderness you will need a tent with a water and windproof outer tent that reaches down to the ground, extra tent pegs and mending material for your tent, a thin ground sheet, a sleeping bag (for use in winter) and toiletries. To be able to cook you will need a camping stove, methylated spirit (or the equivalent), cooking gear, matches, cutlery, cup, detergent and towel. You will carry all the food you will need during the entire tour, as well as everything you will need to drink.

This is more or less the same equipment you need when hiking in the Alps in autumn.

Suggestions for winter tours

If you are planning to go on tours on your own in extremely cold weather and if you are not familiar with an Arctic climate you should avoid doing this in winter on Svalbard. Turn to the local agencies that arrange ski tours, snowmobile tours etc.

Temperatures may even in April and May drop to minus 20° C and in combination with a strong wind the effect of the cold may equal minus 50° C. When going on tours in winter you have to have very warm and windproof clothing. You will need hiking boots (ordinary boots are no good) that can keep the warmth even when it is extremely cold, as well as thermounderwear and sweaters. You will also need a windproof thick cap and very thick, windproof gloves. Your jacket and trousers also have to be very warm and windproof. You should avoid going on tours when it is at its coldest.

Frost Bites and Injuries

It is important to know about the potential risks of frost bites and injuries. If you notice frost injuries you must immediately warm the frozen body part putting on more protective clothing. Never rub the injuried area or pat it with snow!

You can prevent frost bites and injuries by being carefully dressed and always keeping yourself in motion. It is important that you get adequate energy by eating food and snacks that provide extra energy like ordinary sugar, glucose sugar, raisins and nuts. It is also essential to bring some kind of drink on the tours. *Read more in Effects of cold.*

When going on tours or excursions on your own it is important to remember

- never go alone
- bring a weapon and an alarm equipment to scare off polar bears when moving away from the communities
- always report your route to Sysselmannen
- be observant to everything around you, because a polar bear can appear anywhere on the islands
- when camping set out tripwire warning flares around your campsite
- avoid crossing rivers that are ice-cold and often also wide with a strong underwater current
- remember that the ice can not be trusted to walk on in summer
- there are always great risks involved when walking on glaciers
- in summer the surface of the ground has thawed and that is why it may be difficult to walk in some areas; you risk sinking down and getting stuck
- bring adequate equipment depending on the season
- bring a good map and a compass
- bring binoculars
- bring a radio
- bring adequate equipment so that you can be located in case of emergency
- and remember: your mobile phone/ cell phone will not work outside Longyearbyen, Sveagruva and Barentsburg

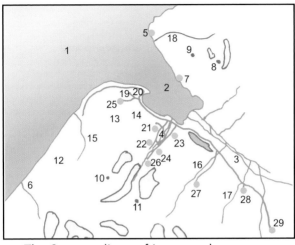

The Surroundings of Longyearbyen

1. Isfjorden
2. Adventfjorden
3. Adventdalen
4. Longyearbyen
5. Revneset
6. Grumant
7. Moskushamn
8. Hiortfjellet
9. Adventtoppen
10. Nordenskiöldfjellet
11. Lars Hiertafjellet
12. Fuglefjella
13. Platåberget
14. Blomsterdalen
15. Bjørndalen
16. Endalen
17. Todalen
18. Hanaskogdalen
19. The Airport
20. The Camp site
21. Mine 1a, 1906-1920
    (The American Mine)
22. Mine 1b 1938-58
    (The Sverdrup mine)
23. Mine 2a
24. Mine 2b (The Santa Claus Mine)
25. Mine 3, 1969-1997
26. Mine 4, 1954-1970
27. Mine 5, 1954-1971
28. Mine 6, 1969-1981
29. Mine 7, 1966-

Common Sense Rules

This is the information Sysselmannen provides on crucial things to keep in mind while visiting Svalbard.

* Never throw litter outdoors.
   Don´t leave any permanent traces after you.
* Don´t disturb the birds and other animals. You are the guest.
* Don´t pick flowers. Regrowth is very slow.
* Don´t destroy or steal cultural remains.
* It is forbidden to approach a polar bear or lure it to you.
   It can be life threatening and the polar bear can also be disturbed.
* Never leave a community without carrying a weapon. You have to know how to use it.
* Show consideration to others.
* Contact Sysselmannen if you plan to leave and stay away some days on your own.
   It is your duty to register your route in most parts of Svalbard.
* Check laws and regulations before you go on tours or other activities.
* For your own sake and that of the environment you should stick to organized tours.
* Sysselmannen can provide you with more detailed information on Svalbard and tourism.

Sysselmannen´s warning of polar bears

It is criminal to follow, lure, feed or disturb polar bears. Any violation of the rules will be prosecuted.

Be well prepared!

To avoid confrontation it is important to prepare carefully and well in advance think about how to conduct yourself in the Svalbard area.

- Be attentive. Look around and move so that you at all times have a general view of the ground around you.
- Move away when you see a polar bear. Never follow it!
-Most polar bears appear when you have pitched your tent. If there are many of you at the camp, sit facing different directions so that you have total control of the area.
- Avoid camping on the shore. Water and ice edges are natural places for polar bears to look for food.
- Use a tripwire around your camp.
- Put food far away from your tent and in such a way that you can keep an eye on it from your tent.
- Never cook food in your tent because polar bears are attracted by the smell of food.
- Never go unarmed. Guns, suited for big-game-hunting (cal. 7.62, 30.06 and 308) and a signal pistol are the appropriate weapons for self-defence against polar bears.

- Make sure you can handle the gun before you go out into the wilderness.

Curious or threatening?

Often a polar bear will approach just out of sheer curiosity. However, all polar bears should be seen as potential threats. As soon as the polar bear has seen you and moves closer towards you, you must try to scare it off at once. Shout and screem, jump and wave your arms. Load your weapon. When the polar bear is closer than 50 metres you should fire a warning shot with the signal pistol at the ground right in front of the polar bear or shoot a warning shot in the air.

To act in self-defence

You have the right to defend yourself against the polar bear. When you have to act in self-defence – in very dangerous situations that you cannot get out of and when you have to protect your own or somebody else´s life, **THEN YOU MUST SHOOT TO KILL!** Aim at the chest and shoot several times. Then approach the polar bear from behind and make sure it is dead.

!!! When you have been forced to kill a polar bear you have to report this to Sysselmannen immeditely.!!!

Special Sights in the Villages

Longyearbyen

There are many interesting things to look at in Longyearbyen. In many places you can see remaining constructions from coal-mining, and you cannot miss the strange Taubanesentralen, the remains of the cableway that was used for the transport of coal. Most of the buildings are situated on the slopes of the southeastern part of the valley, and many houses are painted in garish colours. You also notice that the pipelines are situated above ground so as not to get destroyed by the permafrost. In these pipelines you find the lines for water, sewage and electricity.

In more recent times they have started to dig down these lines in the ground, using a technique that should be able to withstand the movements, caused by the permafrost in this northern region.

*The **Church*** was built in 1958. During the war the Germans burnt down the chapel in use when they laid the communities and the mining premises waste. The church hall contains many interesting details concerning Svalbard´s history. To enter the church hall you pass peisestuen, which is a room where organized cultural activities take place,

and where you also can buy a cup of coffee some evenings and Sundays after morning service.

The minister on Svalbard serves the whole of Svalbard. He makes sure that the Polish scientists at the Polish research station at Hornsund receive visits from a

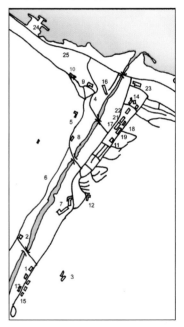

Catholic priest and that the Russian and Ukrainian inhabitants at Barentsburg can attend church services with an Orthodox pope.

Coal mines are found in various places along the mountain sides. You are not allowed to enter any of them due to the risk of collapse and landslides. Left of the church up on the mountain side you find the earliest mine from 1906.

It was here it all began, when the American John Munro Longyear opened his first mine. The mine was called Amerikanergruva, the American Mine, and was closed after a short while. On the same side further into the valley you find Nye gruva 1, also called Sverdrupgruva. On the other side of the valley gruva 2 b is situated, also called Julenissegruva (Santa Claus Mine). Further along the valley to the left you can see the remains of Gruva 2 a.

Many local tour operators arrange guided tours in Gruva 3, that was closed a few years ago and now is used as a Visitor´s Mine. It is situated to the west of Longyearbyen in the mountain above the airport. You should wear warm clothes when visiting the mine, because the temperature there is below zero. Today coal is mined in Gruva 7 that is situated less than 10 km into Adventdalen. Around Longyearbyen there are many closed mines.

Gallery Svalbard is found in Nybyen and has a permanent exhibition of motives from Svalbard by the artist Kåre Tveter. There is also an interesting exhibition of old maps and books, and you can also watch the slide show on "Arctic Light over Svalbard".

The **Graveyard** is situated between the

The entrance at the Santa Claus Mine in Longyearbyen

church and Huset and was opened in 1920. Here victims of the Spanish flu are buried as well as a few dead miners. It is not used for burials today.

Huset (the House) is found at the higher part of the valley and was built after the Second World War. Here there is a restaurant, a cafeteria, a bar and a cinema and also rooms for various groups and organisations.

Before the new church was completed in 1958 church-services were held in the large hall where Saturday night there might be dinner and dance. Early Sunday morning the room was changed into a holy place where mass was read, only to be transformed again into a cinema or something else. It was a real all-purpose-house during those years.

Longyearbyen´s Kunstnersenter is situated in the same building as Gallery Svalbard and is used by guest artists. Here you can follow their work and also buy their products.

Svalbardhallen, the Svalbard Sports hall, has a pool with a sauna, a sports hall, a squash hall, a climbing wall, a shooting-range and other facilities for training. The hall is next to the schoolhouse.

Svalbard Museum is housed in one of the oldest buildings. The exhibition covers the history of whalers and hunters, Svalbard´s geography, geology, plants and animals. You can also study scientific expeditions on Svalbard and events during the Second World War. Outside the museum there is an engine with coal cars.

Sysselmannen´s Office is next to Taubanesentralen in the part of Longyearbyen called Skjæringa. The architecture of the house differs from the rest of the buildings and you cannot miss it. This is Svalbard´s administrative centre, and here you can obtain information of all sorts. Here you also report the trips you intend to make on your own outside the communities.

Taubanen is the cableway that transported coal from the different mines. In the centre of the community there are still well-kept parts of this aerial cableway. Along the mountain sides you can see remainders of it. Nobody can miss seeing a strange, grey building on high legs. That is Taubanesentralen. All cableways were connected here, and from here the coal was taken on a cableway to the coal harbour and loaded on ships for export. On the slope between Taubanesentralen and the centre of Longyearbyen there is a cableway switch where two cableways are joined. Guided tours of Taubanesentralen can be arranged by the museum.

The **War Monument** is situated close to

Cableway

The graveyard from 1920

17

A view of Ny-Ålesund

Sysselmannen´s office. It was raised in memory of the victims on Svalbard during the Second World War.

Ny-Ålesund

Ny-Ålesund has an interesting history, both as a mining community and as a starting point for scientific expeditions. Today it is also a research region for modern and advanced Arctic science.

The *Anchor pylon,* a mast for launching air-ships, stands behind the buildings. From this spot Amundsen in 1926 and Nobile in 1928 started their expeditions to the North Pole.

The *Arctic Research Centre* is on the outskirts of the community close to the mountain side. All measuring and registering equipment of the scientists are found scattered over the grounds. It is forbidden to touch instruments or other scientific material.

High up on the mountain side slightly to the right of the Arctic Research Centre there is a station where tests of carbondioxide and methane gas are

Engine and coal cars from the mines stand close to the harbour and form the northernmost train of the world.

The ***former Hospital*** (a yellow building) is next to the old Post Office.

Kongsbreen is situated at the heart of the fjord and it is a very beautiful glacier. You can follow it far into Spitsbergen where the name is changed to Kronbreen and Kongsvegen.

Kongsfjordbutikken (The Kongsfjord Shop) is the only shop in the community. You can buy postcards here and also get them stamped with the northernmost stamp of the world. You can also buy souvenirs of all kinds, knitted Norwegian sweaters, sealskins etc. Wine, spirit and beer are for sale, but the buyer must bring her/his airline ticket to get the purchase noted on it.

carried out. Here you can also see a camera, facing the community, and thanks to it you are able to follow the weather at Ny-Ålesund on Internet.

Birds breed everywhere, even along roadsides. The birds are protected and must not be disturbed. The Arctic tern is very aggressive if you get too close to her nest with eggs. At Solvattnet, the small lake close to the fjord, and also in the fjord itself there are lots of birds.

The ***Bust of Amundsen*** is found close to the Science Centre.

This train transported coal from the mine to the harbour. It is the northernmost train of the world.

The post office at Ny-Ålesund is today closed and postal services are taken care of by the shop in the community

The **Monuments in Memory of the polar expeditions** are found close to the pylon.

The **Museum** exhibits the history of coal-mining in Ny-Ålesund.

Nordpol Hotellet is the northernmost hotel of the world and was built in the 1930s. It was opened on the 3rd of September 1939, but when people heard of the outbreak of the Second World War it was closed and did not open again until after the end of the war.

The **Ny London houses** are situated close to the harbour and have a very characteristic look. These yellow buildings were moved to Ny-Ålesund after the failure of mining at Ny London on the Blomstrand peninsula across the fjord.

The **old Post Office** is a green little building and is not used today but left as a kind of memorial of the days when Ny-Ålesund had 300 inhabitants and coal-mining was at its peak.

Rules for Visitors to Ny-Ålesund:
All Ny-Ålesund is owned by the former coal-mining company that has issued a number of rules for people visiting at Ny-Ålesund:
* Don´t walk away from the gravel roads
* All breeding birds are protected
* Don´t go too close and don´t touch scientific instruments
* Don´t throw away cigarette butts or litter
* Respect the cultural remains
* Don´t enter houses that are privately owned

Places in Ny-Ålesund

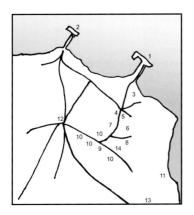

1 New harbour quay
2 Old coal wharf
3 Engine and coal cars
4 Museum
5 Shop and post office
6 Old post office
7 Nordpol Hotellet
8 Old hospital
9 Amundsen´s statue
10 Research stations
11 Anchor pylon for airships
   and North Pole Memorials
12 Kennel
13 Camp site
14 Scientists´ canteen

Kongsfjorden

Many of the streets of Barentsburg are paved with concrete slabs

and is used for producing vegetables.

The *Museum* specializes in minerals. Here they also sell minerals.

The *Poultry farm* is situated close to the farm houses.

Barentsburg

It is advisable to join a guided tour (in English) when coming here. Then you are for instance shown the buildings for self-suffiency and the sports hall. Barentsburg has not the same frequent air connections with Russia as the Norwegian communities have with Norway.

Right from the beginning people here have aimed at being self-supporting by establishing farm-houses with cows and pigs, a poultry farm and a greenhouse.

The whole place is interesting, being so different from Longyearbyen.

Farms with cows and pigs are located to the north part of the community.

The *Green house* is close to the farms

The *Sports hall* offers possibilities for various sports. There is a pool at the hall.

The *Textile factory* provides work for many Russian and Ukrainian women. (The blue house to the left).

The museum at Barentsburg

An ice front in Liefdefjorden

Places of Interest

The tour operators at Longyearbyen arrange visits, tours and boat-trips along the coast. There are lots of offers, and they always include an armed guide, so that you will feel safe from polar bear attacks. If you go on tours on your own you must bring a weapon and be able to use it and above all know how to deal with a polar bear.

The numbers, given in connection with different places, refer to the maps of the areas.

Isfjorden and its Surroundings

1. Adventdalen is a fine example of a so called U-valley. It was formed when a glacier glided through the valley and gave the mountain sides its soft U-form. The river at the bottom of the valley brings along lots of stones and sand and

silt, and the mouth of the river is moved farther away towards Adventfjorden. In summer the area close to the lower part of the river is so watery that it is impossible to walk there. Along the south side of the valley there is a road to Mine 7, less than ten kilometres from Longyearbyen into the valley.

In the valley as well as in many other places on Svalbard there are scientific measuering and registering instruments – both at the bottom of the valley and on the mountain sides. It is forbidden to come near or to touch these instruments.

On the north side of the valley there is a pingo (a hill or a mound consisting of soil and ice) close to the mouth facing Adventfjorden, right across from Longyearbyen. Further into the valley there are two more pingos on the north side. *Read more about pingos in the chapter on Geography and Geology.*

2. Billefjorden is situated at the furthest end of Isfjorden. Here the Russian mining settlement, Pyramiden, once thrived. It was closed after a fire in the mine. There were up to 900 inhabitants in the settlement. On the north side Skansen, the Fort, is situated. It is a mountain of beautiful dark and light layers of stratified rocks.

3. Colesbukta was right up to the 1950s an export harbour for coal, mined by the Russian at Grumant. There are parts of a railway and other remains that tell us about this activity.

4. Coraholmen, the Cora Island, is situated in Ekmanfjorden on the north side of Isfjorden. It was covered by moraine from the Sefströmbreen west of the island in the early 1900s. The east side of Coraholmen still retains the grass covered tundra. The moraine consists of weathered sandstone, that was formed 350 million years ago. Today it is 1.5 to 2 kilometres to the Sefströmbreen and the glacier has

In many places on Svalbard you see old graves

obviously melted that much in less than 100 years.

5. Festningsodden at the mouth of Grønfjorden is interesting because of the discovery of the foot-prints of a dinosaur, belonging to the Iguanodon

Svenskehuset, the Swedish House, at Kapp Thordsen was built in 1870 by a Swedish company, that planned to mine phosphates in the area (10)

family. This animal was 10 to 12 metres long and 3 to 5 metres tall, and the length of the steps was approximately 2 metres. The dinosaur left its marks in damp sand, which later was covered by silt and gradually petrified. These foot-prints are the northenmost ever found of a dinosaur. During the Tertiary period the strata turned vertical. At the end of the 1960s the sandstone steep fell down into the sea, because water had undermined it, and the foot-prints disappeared. In the summer 2004 Norwegian scientists found fossils of an unknown species of a dinosaur.

6. Gipsvika is situated at Sassenfjorden, at the heart of Isfjorden. South of the mouth of Gipselva it has very beautiful shore lines that were formed when the inland ice started to melt in this area 10.000 years ago. The highest shore line is found 75 metres above the surface of the fjord.

7. Grumantbyen, west of Longyearbyen, is a narrow valley with a closed Russian mine.

8. Grønfjorden you find in the south of Isfjorden close to its mouth. On the east side of the fjord the Russian mining community of Barentsburg is found. As late as in the 20th century there were whaling stations in the fjord.

9. Kapp Linné, is situated at the western end of the south side of Isfjorden. Here you find the telecommunication centre for all traffic between Svalbard and Norway. There is also a meteorological station here and a bird reserve along the west coast. As a tourist you can stay and have your meals at the station. There is also a camping site close by.

10. Kapp Thordsen on the north side of Isfjorden is known for Svenskehuset, the Swedish House, built in 1870 by a company owned by among others the Swedish polar scientist A.E. Nordenskiöld. The intent was to mine the phosphates they had discovered. After a more detailed analyses of the find mining was declared uneconomical. 1882-1883 the house was used by a Swedish expedition led by the Swedish meteorologist Nils Ekholm. One of the participants was Andrée, who in 1897 made an attempt to reach the North Pole by balloon.
The house is the oldest on Svalbard and is taken care of by the Norwegian state.

11. Nordenskiöldbreen is a beautiful glacier on Billefjorden.

12. Nordenskiöldfjellet lies close to Longyearbyen and is a more than 1000

metres high mountain and is easy to climb. From the top the scenery is fantastic.

13. Pyramiden in Billefjorden is a former Russian settlement that is not inhabited today. A fire in the mine stopped all work. The name Pyramiden refers to the form of the mountain.

14. Sassendalen is a U-valley identical to Adventdalen. On the east side of the mouth of the valley you find Fredheim, one of the most famous hunting huts on Svalbard. In it Hilmer Nois lived during 39 winters and 50 summers. His wife spent some years there as well. Sysselmannen is responsible for the maintenance of the hut and it is today used as living quarters for guests and scientists.

15. Skansbukta lies on the north side of the mouth of Billefjorden. At the beginning of the 20th century attempts were made to mine gypsum here, but it was difficult to make a profit out of the activity.

16. Tempelfjorden meets the huge ice masses from Von Postbreen, and often the ice breaks and icebergs float away.

16. Templet is a mountain in Sassenfjorden with fine layers of sandstone and flint from the Permian period appr. 275 million years ago. The mountain easily breaks, and the frost weathering creates cracks and fissures. Into these the decomposed material falls down, forming the 200 metres high, beautiful steeps.

17. *Trygghamna* is situated on the north side of Isfjorden close to its mouth. In the past it has been a harbour of refuge in stormy weather. In the 18th century there was also a big Russian whaling station here. You find remains of it today like wooden poles, boards and bricks. There are also Russian graves from this period.

The steam engine was used at the marble mine in Ny London on the Blomstrandhalvøya (19)

The North-Western and the North-ern Parts of Spitsbergen

18. *Amsterdamøya* is found in the northwest corner of Spitsbergen. On the southeast, sandy headland of the island there are rests of the old Dutch whaling station Smeerenburg from the 1700th century.

19. *Blomstrandhalvøya*, the Blomstrand peninsula, is situated on the north side of Kongsfjorden. Here you also find Ny London with remnants of an attempt to mine marble. In the 1910s the Englishman Ernest Mansfield had found marble and obtained financial support in London to start mining and exporting to England. But the marble was of poor quality and the project soon was declared bankrupt.

20. *Bockfjorden* on the west side of Woodfjorden has colourful and beautiful mountain-sides with concentrations of birds on bird rocks. These mountains have a rich vegetation because of all the bird droppings. Here you also find hot springs which are unusual on Svalbard. Far into the fjord there is a mountain called Smørstabben, and at its western edge there are hot springs called Jotunkjeldene. Eight kilometres into the valley there are more hot springs called Trollkjeldene. The

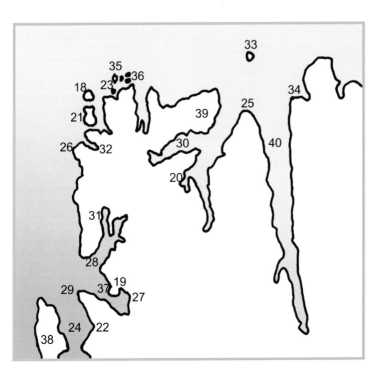

temperature of the water is appr. 24° C. In this valley there is also a pingo facing Bockfjorden and one close to Trollkjeldene.

21. Danskøya was the place where Andrée´s balloon expedition to the North Pole started in 1897. The area is called Virgohamna after the boat that brought people and material to the first launching attempt in 1896. You can still see the rests of Andrée´s expedition but also of the American Wellman´s try in 1906 to 1909 to reach the North Pole by

Three sturdy poles kept the balloon on the ground before the ropes were cut and the balloon rose towards the North Pole (21)

airship.

There are also remains of blubber stoves and the graves of whalers and sailors who died this far north. A monument was raised in 1938 by the Swedish government at the site of the balloon-house. West of the monument, close to the shore, there are the rests of Pike´s house.

The Englishman Pike built it at the end of the 19th century to use it as his basis while hunting in the area. Close to the house there are also parts of the construction that Andrée used when filling his balloon with hydrogen gas. All around the remains of the gas apparatus there are parts of barrels and iron filings. Some metres away from the site of the balloon-house you find poles, put down slantingly and secured to the ground.

Around them the strong ropes of the balloon were tied. On the 11th of July Andrée gave orders that the ropes should be cut and the Eagle, the name he had given the balloon, rose and disappeared towards the north. Not until 33 years later the remains of the expedition were found at Kvitøya. *Read more in the capter Andrée´s North Pole Expedition.*

22. Engelskbukta was the location of an English whaling station in the 1600s.

23. Fair Haven is a strait, pretty well sheltered from the winds between Norskøyane, Fuglesangen, Klovningen, Fugleøya and Spitsbergen. Here whaling ships and other ships could seek shelter from frightening storms.

24. Forlandsundet (the Forland strait) is very shallow and only small boats can pass.

25. Gråhuken has shore banks that are very well formed. In 1872 six Norwegian ships were trapped and confined by drift ice as early as in September. The sailors tried to get help at Nordenskiöld´s scientific post in Mosselbukta, and most of them survived. So did the staff at the scientific post. Seventeen of the younger men managed to reach Svenskehuset at Kapp

Thordsen at Isfjorden where supplies were stored. All seventeen men died during the winter, in spite of plenty of food. The reason was that they did not know how to take precautions against scurvy. They are now buried close to Svenskehuset. Only sixteen graves have been found. The seventeenth man was never buried and now haunts the house, people say.

26. Hamburgbukta is a well sheltered bay on the peninsula south of the inflow into Magdalenefjorden. A German whaling station has been situated here.

27. Kongsfjorden is a very beautiful fjord with broad and spectacular glaciers like Kongsbreen, Kronbreen and Kongsvegen. On the south side of the

fjord lies Ny-Ålesund, where coal mining ceased as early as 1962 and the old coal wharf is abandoned.

28. Krossfjorden is very beautiful and has several small fjords with glaciers. From time to time they are broken at the ice-edge, forming icebergs. On the west side at Ebeltoftbukta there are graves where whalers have been buried.

29. Kvadehuken at the inflow of Kongsfjorden shows a typically structured ground with polygons and circleformed stone configurations. Where the ground slopes down the circles become long ribbons.

30. Liefdefjorden is a lovely fjord with an impressive glacier-front. Here icebergs are broken off and drift in the

Parts of Andrée´s hydrogen gas apparatus (21)

fjord. Usually you see birds on the icebergs, among others kittiwake and ivory gull.

31. Lilliebööksfjorden is surrounded by high, steep mountains and has at its heart a glacier-front that is eight kilometres wide. You notice rests of a German meteorological station from the Second World War.

32. Magdalenefjorden was named by the Basque whalers in the 17th century after the patron-saint of whalers, Saint Magdalena. It is one of the most beautiful fjords on Svalbard. The mountain-sides are steep and the mountains have pointed peaks. Several small glaciers reach the sea here, and icebergs are formed. Once there were many whaling stations here, and there are more than 30 whalers, sailors and others buried here. The graves date from 1650 to 1750 and are found at Gravneset on the south side of the fjord. There is also a memorial to dead whalers, raised by the Norwegian government. On the rocky mountain sides you see large bird colonies.

33. Moffen is a protected, ring-formed island built up by the sea and consists of stone, gravel and sand. Here there is a colony of walruses of varying numbers, from ten to maybe a hun-

dred animals. Often you find them on the south part. The island is also a breeding ground for several species of birds. You are not allowed to go ashore, and you should stay at least 300 metres off the island.

34. Mosselbukta is interesting from the point of Arctic exploration history. Nordenskiöld spent the winter of 1872-73 here, and he was the first Arctic scientist who spent a winter on Svalbard. From this place he went on expeditions and he was the first man to explore parts of Nordaustlandet.

35. Nordvestøyane consist of the islands Norskøyane, Klovningen and Fuglesangen.

At Ny London an attempt was made to mine marble, but it failed (37)

At Moffen there is a large group of walruses

36. Norskøyane are two islands, Inner and Outer Norskøya. On the latter there was a Dutch whaling station in the 17th century, and there are a number of graves from that period. They are said to be 400, but many of them are difficult to locate today.

37. Ny London has rests of a construction for mining marble. The Englishman Ernest Mansfield found marble in the mountain to the south of the peninsula and persuaded many investors in London to stake money on equipment for mining. A small settlement was founded, and machinery of various kinds were shipped here. Houses for workers were built, and two of them still stand while four were moved to Ny-Ålesund to house miners there. When mining began it turned out that the marble was too soft and broke and could not be used at all.

38. Prins Karls Forland is a long, narrow island with faults. The mountains are more than 1000 metres high and have many glaciers. At the north tip of the island, Fuglehuken, there are plenty of large bird colonies. There are often walruses on the north-eastern coast, for example at Murraypynten. During the 18th century a huge amount of whales were killed at the south tip.

39. Reinsdyrflya is a plain where a lot of reindeer graze, up to 1000 animals. You can see polar bears here even in summer, probably because of the reindeer.

At Smeerenburg there was a Dutch whale station in the 1600s.

18. Smeerenburg was the most important Dutch whaling station during the 17th century. At the top of production there were seven double stoves and one single stove here for boiling the blubber. Some stoves had chimneys but most of them had not, and smoke lay thick around them. The products were used as lamp-oil and grease. In its heydays it was a small settlement with dwelling-houses, ware-houses,

handicraft and service of all kinds. In summer the activity was intense. In the autumn everybody returned to Holland but came back next summer. Up to 200 persons worked here at the same time. The work was hard and took place in all kinds of weather. The whales were dragged on to the shore and cut up so that one could get hold of all the blubber and everything else one could use. The remains of the whales were left to decay, and the stench must have been difficult to stand. The men who cut up and boiled the whales were smeared and splashed with fat and oil and stank of blubber and whale-oil. The ground was drowned in oil and fat from time to time. Rain softened the ground and one sank down in sand and a sticky pulp. To solve some of these problems there was a sewage system but it could not keep the ground dry and firm. Those who worked on the whaling-ships and ashore made good money, and there were many men interested in working at Smeerenburg or at other whaling stations.

40. Wijdefjorden is 110 kilometres long, one of the longest on Svalbard. The east side is a fault that continues across the mountains south of the fjord and further on across Billefjorden and Sassenfjorden down towards Sveagruva in the inner part of Van Mijenfjorden. The mountains on both sides of the fjord are high. The east side has a number of small glaciers and narrow, cutdown valleys and is in the inner parts dominated by Svalbard´s highest mountain peaks and many great glaciers.

Hinlopen, the Eastern Coast of Spitsbergen and the Islands East of Spitsbergen

41. Alkefjellet is a bird cliff on the west side of Hinlopen. It consists of basalt that penetrated the limestone during the Jurassic and the Cretaceous periods. You can see the light limestone both above and below the basalt cliffs. The outer basalt cliffs stand as stacks and the birds fly round them like swarming bees. Here are thousands of Brünnich´s

guillemots, ivory gulls and kittiwakes. You can also see tongues of glaciers from Odinjøkulen press forward. Glacier water rushes down between cliffs and stacks, and green moss grows on the damp cliff sides.

49. Andréetangen is a part of the west side of Edgeøya´s south tip and has shore banks. The bedrock is partly basalt. The name Andréetangen comes from a German scientist and has nothing to do with the balloonist Andrée. Here all kinds of birds thrive and even Arctic skua, a bird that forces other birds to throw up their catch in order to get something to eat. Here you also find a house, that up to 1960s was used by hunters and trappers. It is maintained so that scientists can stay and seek shelter in birds, for example ivory gulls that pick small shrimps washed ashore by the waves.

67. Austfonna is the name of the large glacier that covers most of Nordaustlandet, 8400 sq.km. 60% of Svalbard´s total area is covered by

Brünnich´s guillemots crowd together on the shelves of the cliffs (41)

bad weather. Close by there are re-mainders of a building from the days of the Pomors in the 18th century. Pomor was the name of Russian hunters from the White Sea in northern Russia.

43. Augustabukta is a sandy shore on the south-western Nordaustlandet. You can see walruses there, both on land and at sea. On the shore there may also be

glaciers. The ice-area of Austfonna covers 13 % of Svalbard. Along the ice-edge that reaches the sea icebergs are broken off all the time.

44. Barentsøya is a bare island of 1300 sq.km. Almost half of it is covered by a glacier with several tongues of ice reaching the sea.

45. Diskobukta is a longish bay with a great amount of shore banks on the northwestern part of Edgeøya. In the ravines at the mountain-edge of slate there are bird rocks where among other species you find kittiwakes. In ravines like these there may be suitable lairs for Arctic foxes, considering the closeness to food.

46. Dolerittneset is covered by bones from walruses and is found on the north west tip of Edgeøya. It reminds us of the incredible slaughter of walruses that took place in the 18th and 19th centuries. The walruses are very heavy and slow on land, and it was not difficult to club them to death when they lay on the shore resting or sleeping.

There are also buildings here used by scientists. One of the houses is a hexagon, a very rare thing on Svalbard. A few hundred metres further south you see the remains of a house built by the Pomors, the Russian hunters. There are logs and bricks left, and the red bricks tell us it was a Russian house.

47. Edgeøya is an island of almost 5000 sq.km. and as bare as Barentsøya. Half of it is covered by glaciers. In the east the ice reaches the sea, and icebergs are formed. It is an important region for polar bears.

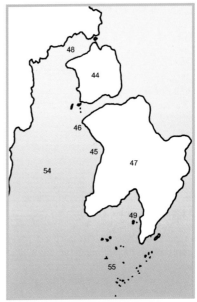

48. Ginevrabotnen between Barentsøya and Spitsbergen is an excellent place for studying polar bears, seals, whales and birds.

42. Hinlopen is the strait between Spitsbergen and Nordaustlandet. Ice conditions in the strait vary in summer but it is generally possible to sail across

The research station at Kinnvika (50)

it in July and August. The problem is that drift ice follows the currents and the winds. In summer the ice moves fast, and one ice-free part of the strait may later be ice-covered. Navigation demands good knowledge of where the ice is and how currents and winds move, but also how conditions will develop during the coming hours or days. On the islands in the south part of the strait there are plenty of seals and polar bears. It is possible to see whales in this region.

Hopen has huge rocks with bird colonies and a meteorological station. Both at Hopen and Edgeøya companies drilled for oil in the 1970s but without any findings. The environment protectionists of Svalbard were relieved because there is a great risk of a conflict between environmental protection and the interests of the oil-companies if oil is found.

50. Kinnvika is situated in the north part of Murchinsonfjorden at the north-western corner of Nordaustlandet. It is a Swedish-Finnish-Swiss research station from 1957/1958. A number of scientists spent a winter here, registrating and investigating various phenomina during the Second Geophysical Year of Science. The station has been used several times during the 1960s and the 1970s. The whole station is maintained, and together with several other science posts it can be opened whenever need arises.

One of the smaller houses was used to register magnetism and the building was nailed together with copper nails. There is not a single iron-filing in the house, because registration would be distorted by iron.

The houses are situated in i gravel and rock plain, an Arctic desert. If you touch the planks on the outer walls you will notice that they have been roughly blasted by the winds. All around there are frost phenomina. Stones and gravel have been lifted up from the ground and arranged in rings. You see parts of slate stand on edge. The largest parts have moved to the furthest side of the ring. There are shore banks that are 10000 years old. They were formed when the land rose and the ocean sank away after the Ice Age.

Kong Karls Land

has beautiful layers of rocks, e.g. sandstone, but also large areas with basalt, that forms hexagonal pillars, protecting lower layers from erosion. The islands are an important region for female polar bears when they are about to give birth.

51. Nordaustlandet is the second largest island of Svalbard with an area of 15193 sq.km. Almost 75% of the area is covered by glaciers, and the largest is Austfonna (8400 sq.km.). The island has an Arctic climate, and it was never of any interest to the whalers or hunters. Winter conditions were too harsh. There are many polar bears and walruses here as well as in all eastern parts of Svalbard. On the drift ice there are many seals of various species.

52. Rijpfjorden, situated on the north coast of Nordaustlandet, is difficult to reach. During the final part of the Second World War Germany had a meteorological station in the south part of the fjord east of Wordieodden. You can see

The German meteorological station from the Second World War at Rijpfjorden (52)

rests of a simple dwelling-house and a ware-house. In 1944 the staff was transported here. They brought all things needed to build the houses, stay the winter and work at the meteorological station. And they also brought

The glacier at Kvitøya with brooks of glacier water

all food needed for a long stay. The weather balloons were filled with hydrogen gas, produced by putting pieces of zinc into sulphuric acid. A radio made it possible for them to keep in contact with German forces and to send weather forecasts.

After the end of the war in May 1945 they sent their weather reports to Norwegian authorities until a Norwegian ship picked them up in September 1945. Then the man in charge of the station gave his revolver to the Norwegian captain as sign of surrender.

53. Sjuøyane, the Seven Islands, lie north of Nordaustlandet and consist of a number of islands. The northernmost one is called Rossøya and on this island Andrée had stored supplies. If the balloon trip to the North Pole would fail, Andrée had stored supplies along the northern coast of Svalbard and also on Franz Josef Land.

The largest island is Phippsøya, and here as well as in many other places on Svalbard Sysselmannen has stored fuel supplies for helicopters and also arranged a shelter in case of bad weather. Walruses and polar bears are usually found in this region.

54. Storfjorden is the sea between Edgeøya and Spitsbergen. The possibilities to see whales, polar bears, walruses, seals and birds are very great.

Storøya east of Nordaustlandet is covered by a glacier in the south. It is a bare island where polar bears stay. They sometimes lie on the glaciers to cool down, and they can look like light yellow-beige or yellow-brownish stones. If you are patient enough to wait the stones may start walking about.

55. Tusenøyane, the Thousand Islands, south of Edgeøya have basalt in the bedrock and you can find very nice examples of hexagonal basalt pillars. There are plenty of walruses here and the birdlife is amazing.

A memorial stone at Kvitøya

56. Vibebukta on the south-western part of Nordaustlandet close to Austfonna is a stone and gravel plain that slowly rises towards land. There are a number of shore lines and it is a good example of an Arctic desert. Among gravel and stones in the banks there are fossils of corals, brachiopods etc. On the shore you find bones from whales, walruses, seals and polar bears. They are drained of nutritive substances, and around the bones several plants can grow.

A memorial pole at Kvitøya

Kvitøya, the White Island, is the most eastern of Svalbard´s islands and is almost totally covered by ice. The island is an important area for polar bears. On the west coast there is an ice-free area of some hundred metres breadth and six to seven kilometres length. The whole shore consists of rocks, stones and gravel. Glacier water flows in small brooks that are covered with green, red and yellow moss. Andrée and his two companions came here after their strenuous walk on the ice, having abandoned their collapsed balloon.

On the rock at the south part of the shore

there is a memorial commemorating the three balloonists: Andrée, Strindberg and Frænkel. Their names are etched on a copperplate, and the plate is cast in a square base of concrete. Close by there is another monument. It dates from 1980 when the Swedish

icebreaker Ymer made an exploration voyage towards the North Pole and also stopped at Kvitøya. It is a rough, wooden pole that has been fixed to the ground, and on its top there is a round slab in memory of Nordenskiöld´s voyage along the North-East passage in 1880 on board the ship Vega and of Ymer´s polar voyage in 1980. The slab is designed by the Swedish artist Gunnar Brusewitz. On the pole there are bite marks of polar bears.
Below the rock with these memorials

the three men tried to pitch their tent. When the camp was discovered in 1930 everything was in a mess, because polar bears had searched it, trying to find something to eat. Everything that remained of the expedition´s equipment is now at the museum in Gränna, Sweden.

The South-Western Part of Spitsbergen

57. Akseløya lies between Bellsund and Van Mijenfjorden and this explains why there are only two narrow passages into Van Mijenfjorden. The island has a bedrock that consists of layers of flintstone. Movement in the earth crust put the layers at edge, and they now stand vertically.

58. Bellsund was visited a long time ago by whalers, hunters and trappers. It offers shelter against west winds. Here there were whaling stations and huts.

59. Brepollen is a many kilometres broad ice-front, formed by Hornbreen, Storbreen and many other glaciers at the heart of Hornsund. It is an amazing experience being surrounded on three sides by glaciers. Now and then ice breaks off, and everywhere in the fjord you see floating icebergs. During the last

mountains and glaciers. Usually there are polar bears all year round at Hornsund. They stay close to the glaciers and on ice floes, floating near the edge of the glaciers.

On the north side of the mouth there is a Polish research station. In winter about ten scientists work there. In summer more scientists join them. This station was established in 1950s.

62. Hornsundtind is the highest mountain peak in the south part of Spitsbergen. It reaches 1431 metres.

60. Luciakammen is a narrow and high mountain ridge at a

decades this glacier front has melted and drawn back almost two kilometres.

60. Burgerbukta on the north side of Hornsund is a place where you often see big icebergs breaking off from the glaciers that reach the bay.

61. Hornsund is a very beautiful and interesting fjord. The mountains have pronounced peaks with glaciers in between. In particular the south side offers stunning sceneries of steep

Odd Ivar Ruud´s hut at Sofiebogen (60)

43

height of more than 900 metres. Here as well as on Sofiekammen there are huge bird colonies of guillemots, little auks and kittiwakes. The glacier between these two ridges reaches the fjord and icebergs break off and float out into the fjord.

60. Sofiebogen is a huge cliff that raises vertically to a height of 600 metres. At the ridge Sofiekammen there are lots of birds on the shore and on the rocks. The most remote part of the ridge soars 900 metres. In previous times there have been hunters here. Odd Ivar Ruud´s hut is still standing, and it is interesting to enter and see how men like him lived long ago on Svalbard.

Cloudy mountains at Hornsund (61)

Spitsbergen was named by the Dutch discoverers in 1596 after the pointed mountains they found along the west coast. The official name of this northern group of islands is Svalbard.

63. Stormbukta is a bay, difficult to reach. The coast here is full of rocks and sub-merged banks, and it can be next to im-possible to come ashore. The name, Bay of Storms, was given to the place because very cold and strong winds rage down from the east over the glaciers. The shore is also exposed to the winds from the Atlantic, and it has a high shore bank created by the gales. Higher up on the shore there are older shore banks.

On the rocks you find kittiwakes and also blue foxes, a variety of the Arctic fox. The bedrock consists of limestone, and the glacier water has created subterranean streams that reach the sea. In the south part there is a hot spring. There has also been a German mete-orological station here but now there are few remainders of it.

64. Sveagruva, the Svea Mine, is found at the heart of Van Mijenfjorden north of Sveabukta. Coal seams are up to five metres broad, and the area is considered to be the largest coal deposit on Svalbard.

Sofiebogen (60)

Bautaen at Hornsund (61)

65. *Torbjørnsenfjellet* is a mountain with bird rocks, densely populated by little auks.

66. *Van Mijenfjorden*, and particularly the inner part of it, is a home for seals. There are also huge moraine formations from earlier glaciers here. At the northernmost end of Sveabukta there is the Sveagruva, a very rich coal deposit.

Useful
Information

(If nothing else is stated the information refers to Longyearbyen.)

A

Accomodation. See Camping, Hotels and Youth Hostels.

Arms. You have to be armed while staying outside the communities because of the risk of encountering polar bears.

B

The **Bank** is located at the centre and offers all kinds of services. An ATM machine is found at the entrance of the bank.

Bars: Huset, Karls-Berger Pub, Kroa, Radisson SAS Polar Hotel Spitsbergen and Spitsbergen Hotel.

Beer, spirit and wine are for sale at Svalbardbutikken and at the shop at Ny-Ålesund. You have to bring your airline ticket so that your purchase can be stamped on it.

Bike. You can rent a bike at Basecamp Spitsbergen, Poli Arctici, Spitsbergen Guesthouse and Radisson SAS Polar Hotel Spitsbergen.

Biological processes are very slow on Svalbard. That is why you have to protect the environment.

Blood-alcohol percentage. 0.02 % is the legal limit of blood-alcohol percentage while driving any motor-vehicle.

Boat tours are arranged from June until the middle of September.

Books on Svalbard are sold in many shops, at the Tourist Information, the Svalbard Museum and in the receptions at the hotels.

"Busen" was the name of the miner and he is represented by a statue at the centre of Longyearbyen. There is also a statue of a miner who drills lying down.

C

Camping. In Longyearbyen camping is only allowed at the camp site close to the airport and at Ny-Ålesund south-east of the community beyond the anchor pylon. At Kapp Linné, Sveagruva and the Polish research station in Hornsund you have to get permission by the one who is in charge of the place. Everywhere else camping is allowed – but not in protected areas and bird reserves and closer than 100 metres from cultural remains.

Charge card and **credit card** generally can be used.

The **church** is open to visitors and in peisestuen different activities are organized. You can also have a cup of coffee or tea there.

Cinema. There is a cinema at Huset.

Climate. Svalbard has a high Arctic climate. It is cold, windy and dry which turns Svalbard into an Arctic desert. In Longyearbyen the midnight sun is visible from 21st of April to the 21st of August – and the polar night reigns from the 28th of October to the 14th of February. The average temperature in summer is +6° C and in winter -14° C. The heavy winds can make you feel much colder.

Clothing. In summer you need the same clothing as while walking in the Alps in the autumn. You also need rainwear and you can use ordinary shoes in the communities, but in the wilderness you need hiking boots or rubber boots. In the winter the temperature can drop to -30° C and the winds can be heavy. *Read more in the chapter Facts for Visitors.*

Coffee bars. Basecamp Spitsbergen, Fruene Kaffe & Vinbar, Gallery

Svalbard, Huset, Kafé Busen and Kroa.

Cultural activities. The church offers services and different activities in peisestuen. At Huset there is a cinema and various other cultural events are also hosted. At Nybyen there is Gallery Svalbard with a permanent exhibition of works by Kåre Tveter, a slide show "Arctic Light over Svalbard", an exhibition of antique maps and books and various other exhibitions. You can also buy art and handicraft there.

A **Cultural remain** is the term used about all remains of human activity before 1946. Both moveable and immoveable items are protected. In a zone of 100 metres around a cultural remain you are not allowed to camp or light a fire.

Currency. The unit of currency is the Norwegian crown, used even at Barentsburg.

D

Dentist. There is a dentist at the hospital. Phone nr 113.

Dogsledding is organized by Svalbard Villmarkssenter.

Duty to report concerns the tourists who would like to go on tours of their own on Svalbard. You report at Sysselmannen´s office. An area around Longyearbyen, Sveagruva and Barentsburg plus an area around Ny-Ålesund are excepted. But Sysselmannen wants reports to be entered whenever you plan to leave the communities.

E

Electricity. On Svalbard 220 V is used.

Equipment necessary on tours is found at Svalbard Reiser and Svalbard Snøscooterutleie.

F

Firearms are rented at Sportscenteret in Lompensenteret, Svalbard Arctic Sport, Svalbard Reiser, Svalbard Snøscooterutleie, Svalbard Wildlife Service and Svalbardbutikken.

Fossils are sold in some shops, but fossil-tours are also organized.

Furs, including polar bear, and sealskins are sold at Skinnboden Arctic Products.

H

Hairdresser. There is a hairdresser at Lompensenteret.

Horseback riding. You can rent an Icelandic horse at Svalbard Hestesenter close to the air-port.

Hotels. The two hotels are Radisson SAS Polar Hotel Spitsbergen and Spitsbergen Hotel.

Hunting and fishing are strictly regulated on Svalbard. The tourist agencies and Sysselmannen can give you more information.

Huset is situated far into the valley on the same side of the river bed as the church and the museum. Here there are rooms for various activities and even cinema, a restaurant, a news-stand and a pub.

I

Information for tourists is available at Info Svalbard/Svalbard Reiseliv.

L

Library. There is a library at Lompensenter.

Litter. You are not allowed to throw litter outdoors. You should put it in garbage containers in the communities.

The **local newspaper,** Svalbardposten, is published on Fridays and provides information on future events, for instance coming movies. You can buy it in some shops.

M

Maps are sold at Norsk Polarinstitutt at Næringsbygget, Skinnboden Arctic Products, Svalbard Reiseliv/Svalbard Tourism and Svalbardbutikken.

Mobile Phones/cell phones can only be used in Longyearbyen, Sveagruva and Barentsburg.

Moped. You can rent a moped at Spitsbergen Guesthouse.

The **museum** is situated close to the church and houses exhibitions on geology, history of mining etc. Outside the museum there is an engine with coal cars.

P

Pharmacies. There is no pharmacy or drugstore on Svalbard but Svalbardbutikken sells some nonprescription drugs. Contact the hospital if you need prescription drugs.

The **Polar bear** is protected and you can come across it anywhere. As a rule you can feel safe in the communities in summer. In winter polar bears are found all over Svalbard. In some places along the west coast you see polar bears in summer, for instance in the north-west region and at Hornsund. Polar bears regard human beings as food, and you must be armed when moving outside the communities. If you meet one you have to try to scare it off but if it attacks you must shoot to kill it.

Police. You can contact the local police at Sysselmannen´s office. Phone number 112.

Post office. There is a Post Office at the centre offering all kinds of postal services. In Ny-Ålesund the Post Office is in the shop.

Prices. Svalbard is a duty-free zone, and most things are cheaper than on the Norwegian mainland. Beer, spirit and wines are considerably cheaper. Fresh goods of all kinds are more expensive because of the costs of transportation.

R

Rabies, a lethal disease for human beings, is found on Svalbard among dogs, polar bears, Arctic foxes, reindeer and seals. Never touch living or dead wild animals!

Restaurants you can find at Huset, Kafé Busen, Kroa, Radisson SAS Polar Hotel Spitsbergen and Spitsbergen Hotel.

Rotary. There is a Rotary club in Longyearbyen. Meetings at the Spitsbergen Hotel every Monday at 06.30 pm.

S

Shoes. You take off your shoes on entering public offices, libraries, hospitals, some restaurants, bars and shops. The reason for this is the fact that shoes or boots can be dirty, having been exposed to filth in the streets. It is partly a tradition, dating back to the old coal-mining days when coal-dust was abundant and stuck to shoes and boots.

Shops.
Lompensenteret has shops where you can buy clothing, shoes, souvenirs, film, crystal, sweaters, flowers etc.

Sport equipment is found at Arctica, Sportscenteret at Lompensenteret and Svalbard Arctic Sport.

Svalbardbutikken sells food, clothes, electrical articles, photo equipment, maps, cosmetics, jewellery, pharmaceutical articles, souvenirs, beer, spirit and wines.

Smoking is forbidden in all public places and at the air-port.

Snowmobiles can be rented at Henningsen Transport & Guiding, Svalbard Snøscooterutleie and Svalbard Reiser. The season lasts from October to May.

Stamps are sold at the Post Office and at many shops.

Statues. In the centre there is a statue of "Busen", the classic Svalbard miner and a statue of a miner who is working lying down in a mine shaft.

Svalbardposten, the local newspaper, appears every Friday.

T

Taxi service is provided by Longyearbyen Taxi AS, tel 7902 1375

and Svalbard MaxiTaxi tel 7902 1305.

Telephone. There are public telephones in Longyearbyen.

Tipping. Tips are given to taxi drivers and in restaurants.

Tourist information is provided by Info Svalbard/Svalbard Reiseliv.

Tours, trips and treks are arranged by local tour operators.

Weapon you can hire at Sportcenteret in Lompensenteret, Svalbard Arctic Sport, Svalbard Reiser, Svalbard Snøscooterutleie, Svalbard Wildlife Service and Svalbardbutikken.

Youth hostels do not exist but there are possibilities of inexpensive lodgings for instance at Basecamp Spitsbergen, Gjestehuset 102, Mary-Ann´s Polarrigg and Spitsbergen Guesthouse.

Addresses, Phone numbers, Fax, Web-sites and e-mail

With reservation of any alterations

All addresses of Longyearbyen:
N-9171 Longyearbyen, Norway.
Country code of Norway: 47.
Below is P = Phone, M = mobile
and F = Fax.

SOS Emergency Phones

Fire	110
Doctor	113
Police	112

Governor of Svalbard (Sysselmannen)

Office hours	79 02 43 00
Outside office hours	79 02 12 22
Casualty clinic	79 02 42 00

LONGYEARBYEN

Services

Bank, P:7902 2910, F:7902 2911

Hospital, P:7902 4200. Dentist: P:7902 4230

Norwegian Polar Institute (Norsk Polarinstitutt), P.O. Box 505, P:7902 2600, F:7902 2604, www.npolar.no, nps@npolar.no

Post Office, P:7902 1604

Svalbard Church, P:7902 1320

Svalbard Reiseliv, P.O. Box 323, P:7902 5550, F:7902 5551, www.svalbard.net, info@svalbard.net

Svalbard Rotary Club, meeting at Spitsbergen Hotel Monday 06:30 pm.

Sysselmannen (Governor of Svalbard), P:7902 4300, F:7902 1166, www.sysselmannen.svalbard.no, firmapost@sysselmannen.svalbard.no

UNIS, P.O. Box 156, T:7902 3300, F:7902 3301, www.unis.no, post@unis.no

Travel Agents, Tour Operators and Accomodation

Arctic Adventures AS, P.O. Box 480, P:7902 1624; M:415 26 121, F: 7902 1745, www.arctic-adventures.no, info@arctic-adventures.no

Arctic Buss og Båttransport, (trips by boat or bus), P.O. Box 171, P:7902 1112, M:913 51 927, F: 7902 1113

Basecamp Spitsbergen, P.O. Box 316, P:7902 4600, F:7902 4601, www.basecampexplorer.com, bookingsvalbard@basecampexplorer.com

Gjestehuset/Guesthouse 102, P/F:7902 5716, www.wildlife.no, 102@wildlife.no

Henningsen Transport & Guiding (snowmobile), P.O. Box 353, P:7902 1311, M:918 53 756, F:7902 1882, www.longyearbyen.net/farm, htg@longyearbyen.net

Longyearbyen Camping, P.O. Box 6, P:7902 1068, 7902 1444, F:7902 1067, info@longyearbyen-camping.com

Mary-Ann´s Polarrigg, P.O. Box 17, P:7902 3702, F:7902 1097, riggen@longyearbyen.net

Nox Polaris (tours), P.O. Box 555, P/F:7902 1869, M:911 09 753, www.nox.no, nox@longyearbyen.com

Poli Arctici, P.O. Box 89, P:7902 1705, M:913 83 467, F:7902 1734, www.poliarctici.com, stefano@poliarctici.com

Radisson SAS Polar Hotel Spitsbergen, P.O. Box 554, P:7902 3450, F:7902 3451, www.spitsbergentravel.no, sales.longyearbyen@radissonsas.com

Spitsbergen Guesthouse, P:7902 6300, F:7902 6301, www.spitsbergentravel.com, spitsbergen.guesthouse@spitsbergentravel.no

Spitsbergen Hotel, P.O. Box 500, P:7902 6200, F:7902 6201, www.spitsbergentravel.no, hotel@spitsbergentravel.no

Spitsbergen Tours, P.O. Box 6, P:7902 1444, 7902 1068, F:7902 1067, www.longyearbyen-camping.com, info@terrapolaris.com, info@longyearbyen-camping.com

Spitsbergen Travel, P.O. Box 548, P:7902 6100, F:7902 6101, www.spitsbergentravel.com, info@spitsbergentravel.no

Svalbard Airport, P:7902 4770, F:7902 1728, svalbard@lufttransport.no

Svalbard Auto, P.O. Box 236, P:7902 4930, F:7902 4931

Svalbard Explorer, P.O. Box 412, P:7902 1149, M:907 62 933, F:7902 3977, www.svalbardexplorer.no, info@svalbardexplorer.no

Svalbard Hestesenter (riding), P.O. Box 182, P:7902 3595, M:917 76 595, F:7902 1233, svalbard.hestesenter@longyearbyen.net

Svalbard Huskies, P.O. Box 543, P/F:7902 5780, M:984 04 089, www.svalbardhuskies.com, info@svalbardhuskies.com

Svalbard Nature, P.O. Box 594, P:+33 4 764 13 840, F:+33 4 764 13 841

Svalbard Reiser (snowmobile tours), P.O. Box 433, P:7902 5650, F:7902 5651, johansl@online.no

Svalbard Snøscooterutleie (snowmobile), P.O. Box 538, P:7902 1666, F:7902 1771, www.scooterutleie.svalbard.no, post@scooterutleie.net

Svalbard Tourism, P.O. Box 323, P:7902 5550, F:7902 5551, www.svalbard.net, info@svalbard.net

Svalbard Villmarkssenter, P.O. Box 396, P:7902 1985, M:907 90 076, F:7902 1986, www.svalbard-adventure.com, villmarkssenter@longyearbyen.net

Svalbard Wildlife Service, P.O. Box 164, P:7902 5660, F:7902 5661, www.wildlife.no, info@wildlife.no

Taxi: Longyearbyen Taxi, P: 7902 1375, M:918 33 462 and Svalbard MaxiTaxi, P: 7902 1305

NY-ÅLESUND

Kings Bay AS, 9173 Ny-Ålesund, P:7902 7200, F:7902 7201

MUSEUM

Svalbard Museum, P.O. Box 521, P:7902 1384, F:7902 1344, post@svalbardmuseum.no

Ny-Ålesund Museum, 9173 Ny-Ålesund

Grenna Museum, P.O. Box 104, Brahegatan 38-40, 56322 Gränna, Sweden, P:0390 41010, 0390 41015, F: 0390 10275 www.grm.se/grennamuseer, andree@grm.se

Climate

Svalbard has a high Arctic climate, it is cold, windy and dry which turns Svalbard into an Arctic desert. The average temperature is +6° C in summer and -14° C in winter. Svalbard is situated in between 1100 and 1500 kilometres from the North Pole. Considering its northern latitude it has a more temperate climate than corresponding northern regions in Russia, Canada or Greenland. The Gulf Stream reaches the sea around Svalbard and southern and southwestern winds bring warm air from the Atlantic Ocean. The west coast of Spitsbergen has the most temperate climate while the eastern parts of Svalbard are more dominated by cold Arctic currents from the east and north.

The precipitation is low on Svalbard but varies in different regions. In the west there falls 200-400 mm per year, in the east at least 1000 mm per year – based on observations of the snow-depth on glaciers.

In winter ice conditions are difficult, and only the west coast might be ice-free. The fjords freeze over and drift ice appears from the north and the east. Even in summer Hinlopen, the strait between Spitsbergen and Nordaustlandet, may be packed with drift ice, and that makes it impossible to sail around Spitsbergen and Nordaustlandet.

Arctic currents and winds influence the movements of the drift ice and conditions are very changeable. There are stories about boats, caught in the drift ice because of rapid changes in the weather.

Summer is short and breezy. In the summer the sun melts the snow, and plants begin to grow, sometimes while still being in the snow. The bird rocks are centres of intense activity. Along the shores and other coastal areas you can see waders and geese. Summer is a hectic time for plants and animals. The streams are filled with glacier water. They are pretty wide and the water is ice-cold. The current is strong, and after a rain the water level rises fast. You should avoid crossing them. In July and August thousands of tourists visit Svalbard, arriving by boat or plane.

Latitude	Midnight sun from	to	No of days	Polar night from	to	No of days
77°	24/4	18/8	117	31/10	11/2	104
78°	21/4	21/8	123	28/10	14/2	110
79°	18/4	24/8	129	25/10	17/2	116
80°	15/4	27/8	135	22/10	20/2	122

Hornsund 77°N, Barentsburg and Longyearbyen just north of 78°N, Ny-Ålesund 79°N and the north coast of Spitsbergen 80°N.
The period of midnight sun is almost two weeks longer than the period of polar night. The rays of the sun are slightly bent down during the passage through the atmosphere of the earth, and that makes it possible for us to see the sun even if it has sunk below the horizon.

Autumn comes in September, and the landscape changes into a red, orange and yellow world. The days grow shorter, temperature falls, the ground freezes and the snow returns. This gives the mountains a different look and they become more "graphic" in their appearance. The frozen ground is easy to walk on, the air is crystal clear and the sun is sinking slowly. In October it has disappeared completely below the horizon.

Winter is a hard time, and it is dark. The polar night lasts from the end of October to the middle of February. On a clear night when you see the stars and the moon there is at least some light. A full moon lasts several days and nights. And now you can experience the absolutely incredible northern lights, the aurora borealis. It shines, sparkles and rolls in the sky. Many people consider February to be the best part of the year. Then light slowly returns and the blue shades of

Adventdalen

the sky are mixed with pink tones. The landscape is tinged with shades of blue and pink.

Spring means longer days. In April the midnight sun appears, and the days are beautiful. The fjords are still frozen and there is still snow on the ground. Migratory birds return and start breeding. On the ice you can see seals basking the sun. Now it is nice to go exploring on skis and snowmobiles. The period between the end of March and the end of April is perfect for winter tours. But it can be cold, and the winds make the cold even more fierce. Right onto the middle of June you can go on glacier tours. In May and June severe cold is not common. But in the valleys snow and ice have begun to melt, and it can be risky and difficult to try to go there.

Read more about wind and temperature on the pages 124 and 125.

Even in summer there is drift ice north of Svalbard

Geography and Geology

Svalbard and Spitsbergen

The name Svalbard is found in the old Icelandic manuscripts. There is a statement from 1194 A.D., "Svalbardi fundin", Svalbard has been discovered. Men from Iceland also seem to have sailed to "the cold coast", the literal meaning of the name Svalbard. There are directions

Position

Svalbard lies between latitudes 76° and 81° N and longitudes 10° and 35° E north of Norway's northern tip. Hornsund lies on latitude 77°, Barentsburg and Longyearbyen just north of latitude 78°, Ny-Ålesund on latitude 79° and the north coast of Spitsbergen just north of latitude 80°. Bjørnøya is also a part of Svalbard, appr. 200 km south of Svalbard.

Geography

Svalbard measures 63.000 sq.km., and 60% of the archipelago is covered by glaciers. In particular the eastern part is dominated by large glaciers. The largest is Austfonna in Nordaustlandet with an ice front of 200 km on the ocean. In the west where the warm water of the Gulf Stream and south and south-west winds determine the climate there are large, almost ice-free areas. But in winter even the west coast may be frozen.

Svalbard consists of a number of islands. Often Svalbard is called Spitsbergen, the name of the largest and best-known island. On this island you find all the existing communities. Most visitors to Svalbard go to the different parts of Spitsbergen's west and northwest coast. Here you find lots of interesting regions.

how to sail from Iceland to Svalbard in four days.

At the end of the 1600th century Dutch sailors named this group of islands Spitsbergen because of the pointed peaks they saw when sailing along the west coast of the island Spitsbergen. In 1920 Norway gained the sovereignty over the islands and Svalbard became the official name.

Along streams and brooks you find moss

bedrock.

But you also find plateau mountains where the plateau is elevated to a height of 500-600 metres. In the east region there are more stratified rocks from different periods in the history of earth.

All Svalbard has permafrost down to 150-300 metres; the ground is always frozen apart from the uppermost layer that thaws in summer. This is the reason why it may be difficult to walk in certain areas in summer; the ground is changed into a pulp. When building a house you have to drive poles into the permafrost, so that the house will not start moving when it freezes in winter and thaws in summer. Poles of spruce or pine wood will do, because

The east part of this Arctic archipelago offers a very wild, cold and partly inaccessible country. But it is well worth visiting even if it is not as easy to reach as the west coast of Spitsbergen. It is in the eastern part of Svalbard you have the greatest opportunities to see polar bears, whales, walruses and seals as well as many bird colonies.

The landscape of Svalbard is formed by the Ice Age and the glaciers. There are fjords and beautiful U-formed valleys, created by the movements of the glaciers. Mountains that have not been cut down by the ice stand as pointed peaks against the sky. Particularly the west coast is rich in many and steep mountains, composed of eruptive and transformed

Polygon ground

The highest mountain peaks
Newtontoppen (northeastern Spitsbergen)   1717 m
Perriertoppen (northeastern Spitsbergen)   1717 m

Some facts about Svalbard

Region	Area sq.km.	Glaciers sq.km.	Glaciers %	Number of glaciers
Spitsbergen	38612	21767	56,4	1598
Nordaustlandet	15193	11309	74,7	210
Edgeøya	5230	2130	40,7	110
Barentsøya	1321	575	43,5	126
Kvitøya	710	705	99,3	1
Prins Karls Forl	622	83	13,4	33

The area of some glaciers (sq.km.)

Austfonna (Nordaustlandet)	8412
Olav V Land (eastern Spitsbergen)	3000
Vestfonna (northwestern Nordaustlandet)	2505
Åsgårdsfonna (northeastern Spitsbergen)	1645
Edgeøyjøkulen (Edgeøya)	1300
Barentsøyjøkulen (Barentsøya)	571
Kronebreen (northwestern Spitsbergen)	693

in these Arctic regions there are no bacteria that can destroy the wood. At the airport permafrost has caused problems on the landing strip. To prevent permafrost in the ground from thawing, stones were used as filling material under the landing strip. But the filling could not prevent movements in the foundation in summer. To reduce the effect of the sun and eliminate the risks of thawing under the filling material, the landing strip was painted white. When realizing that this was not enough new filling and new paving were added. In spite of this there are still movements

Stratified rocks, formed by movements in the earth crust

in the foundation, probably due to the existence of water under the landing strip.

Frost movements of soil, sand and stones can also form more or less hexagonal or round patterns on the ground, called polygon ground or square ground. It is fairly common to see flat stones stand on edge in such patterns. On hill sides the squares can form ribbons of stones or gravel. In some places there is a different kind of permafrost formations. They are strangely rounded or conical heaps on the ground. The formation is called a pingo and it is found in permafrost regions. The pingo is built up from mineral soil, and has a core of ice. The shape is caused by subsoil water under pressure. It forces its way through weak zones in the frozen ground. Sometimes it has a crater-shaped top, because the ice of the core melts and the pingo crumbles at the top.

Geology

Svalbard is situated on the outer edge of the European continental plate. West and north of Svalbard the bottom of the sea steeps down to great depths. Some parts of Svalbard were formed at the same time as the Norwegian-Swedish mountain ridge appr. 400 million years ago when edges of the two tectonic plates, the North American and the European met. As the plates slowly move apart today volcanic activity is freed and lava erupts through cracks between the plates. At the bottom of the Atlantic Ocean the mid-Atlantic ridge was formed, stretching from the Arctic Ocean to the south of the Atlantic. Iceland and Jan Mayen were created as well as the Azores and Tristan da Cunha in the southern part of the Atlantic.

Svalbard is a place where rocks are found from all the geological periods of the earth, a heaven for geologists. In many areas you find fossils from different geological periods, for instance rests of plants, shells, ammonites, trilobites and corals.

Fossil tree trunk

Both tracks and fossils of dinosaurs have also been found. During several of the geological periods coal was formed. Today it is mined both by Norwegian and Russian coal companies.

Svalbard has been exposed to various movements in the earth crust, and because of this there are many faults. One of them is found along the east

Basalt cliffs at Alkefjell

side of Wijdefjorden and continues down in the direction of Sveagruva in the inner part of Van Mijenfjorden. There are even some hot springs on Svalbard. They are situated at the heart of Bockfjorden in northwestern Spitsbergen and southwards along a fault on the east border of Bockfjorden. Hot springs have also been found on the west coast, for the last 40.000 years. Land covered by the ice sheet is pressed down by the weight of the ice, and when the ice melts the land raises again. In Sweden this is obvious at Höga Kusten, Ångermanland, a well-known Swedish World Heritage. You can see old shore lines on the west coast of Svalbard as well as in the fjords at Gipsvika, Sassenfjorden and at Vibebukta on

The moraine at Coraholmen was formed by the glacier on the left

example at Stormbukta, north of Sørkapp.

During all the glacial periods that have existed in the northern hemisphere even Svalbard has been ice-covered. According to some scientists the west and north coasts may have been free from the continental ice sheet during

southwestern Nordaustlandet.

Many of the glaciers change, sometimes they grow and sometimes they are diminished. A good example of this is the glaciers at Hornsund. In just a few years these glaciers melted so dramatically that the ice-front shrunk back two kilometres. Changes like these are difficult to explain. Of two adjoining glaciers one of them can melt and lessen its volume and size while the other grows and pushes its ice-front forward.

An other example of these changes is Sefströmbreen at Ekmanfjorden to the north of Isfjorden. At the beginning of the 20th century this glacier grew fast and amassed lots of gravel from the 350 million years old bedrock of Old Sandstone. The ice-front reached Coraholmen (the Cora Island) in Ekmanfjorden and there a moraine was formed of the red bedrock gravel. Before this the island was covered with grass. The eastern part of the island is still grass-covered tundra, because the movement of the glacier was stopped before the whole island was turned into a moraine. After this Sefströmbreen melted drastically, and the ice-front shrunk back. Today it is found almost two kilometres west of Coraholmen.

Glacier water runs down into cracks in the glacier ice and forms a stream under the glacier. The water of the glacier stream is sweeter and lighter than the water of the fjord, so it soars upwards and melts the ice from under. A jökulport, a glacier gateway, is created at the mouth of the stream into the fjord.

Plants and Animals

Plants

Svalbard´s bedrock, the morphology of the landscape and the climate are the basic conditions for all vegetation. There is often a strip of flat land from 100 metres to several kilometres wide along the coasts. And it is on this flat shore that most of the activity is found and where the biological production is at its most.

Small variations of the topography can affect the vegetation greatly. A slight difference in height can decide whether a plant will strike root and grow and survive – or not.

The thickness and location of the snow is important as well as how sheltered against the winds a habitat of a plant is. The ground humidity and the frost movements are also of importance for all vegetation.

Because of low temperature and low bacteria activity there are limited resources of phosphates, nitrates and other important minerals. But in places where these nutritive substances are found there is a very rich flora indeed, in particular around bird rocks and on shores where there are bones, remains of the slaughter of walruses and whales.

The vegetation layer is very thin and extremely fragile, sensitive to wear and tear. The highest plants reach 15 centimetres, but the most common species only reach one or two centimetres, creeping close to the ground. There are appr. 160 species excluding all moss, lichen and algae. The Svalbard flora is almost identical to the one in the Norwegian and Swedish mountains. Some species are not seen in the Scandinavian mountains but occur on Svalbard and in the Arctic Russia, Alaska and Canada. There are neither trees nor bushes on Svalbard.

The cold climate gives the plants a season of only 1.5 to 2.5 months. Some species sprout through the snow in the late spring and bloom only a few days after the snow has melted. It is essential to go to seed during the short season, and some plants have their own methods to succeed. There are grasses that fructify themselves and create a new plant in their spikes. This new plant falls to the ground and strikes root immediately. Other plants produce sprout buds that fall to the ground and root.

Mammals

The polar bear is one of the largest
predators of the world and King of
Svalbard. This huge animal roams all
over Svalbard in winter, but in
summer you find him in the eastern
regions. The polar bear regards man as
a prey and you have to be very careful
while staying outside the
communities. You have to be armed.
But polar bears can also move into the
communities so you must always pay
attention to your surroundings.

A full-grown female can weigh up to
400 kilos and a male up to 700 kilos. In
spite of their sizes they are very fast
and agile.
As a rule the polar bear feeds on seals
and their young ones, but it can also
try to find food in huts and houses.
Having broken down doors or
windows the polar bear gets inside
and devours whatever it finds. The
polar bear is said to be able to open
tin cans without hurting itself. In the
summer 2001 a female with two cubs

entered the houses at Sveagruva and ate what she found. These bears were later shot with anaestethic capsules, and flown to Edgeøya on the east coast. The same summer some Swedish tourists discovered that they had had a visitor in their tent. The polar bear had eaten their toothpaste but ignored the ham hanging in the tent.

In December the female generally gives birth to two cubs but she stays hibernating until March. By then she has lost a lot of weight and is quite thin. Her weight may be more than a hundred kilos less than in August. The cubs stay with their mother for two and a half years, and when they have left her she copulates again.

Arctic foxes are found all over Svalbard. They are very shy and their white fur makes it difficult to discover them in winter. But in summer their fur is brownish and they are easier to spot. If you are really lucky you can see blue fox, a variety

of the Arctic fox. Its fur is bluish grey to dark brown all year. The Arctic fox has the thickest fur of all mammals. Its lair is hidden in a rock, and the male and the female form lifelong relationships. The cubs are born in May and can survive on their own as early as in July or August.

The Arctic fox needs a hunting-ground of 20 to 25 sq.km. and feeds on seabirds, geese and ptarmigans and can also eat young seals and carcasses.

Its thick fur and its ability to store fat

during late summer and autumn help it to cope with harsh winter conditions. It also hoards animals of prey, but in winter it probably keeps very still in its lair to save energy.

The Svalbard reindeer is smaller than its mainland relative with shorter legs and a more shaggy coat. It is supposed to be related to reindeer found in northern Canada. It roams the islands and can also be seen in the communities. In winter it stays on mountain ridges where the wind has swept away the snow and where it is easier to graze. In summer it is found on the grass covered tundra.

The harp seal frequents the drift ice and pack ice in summer and goes south in winter.

The hooded seal prefers the sea but in summer it can be seen north of Spitsbergen and Nordaustlandet in the drift ice.

The harbour seal is found around Prins Karls Forland, the northernmost region for this kind of seal. You often see it on windsheltered rocks or shores with pebbles or gravel.

Grazing reindeer on the outskirts of Ny-Ålesund

Seals

There are many different species of seals along the coast of Svalbard and at sea. The young ones are born in late winter and are often hidden under snow and ice. Both full-grown seals and their young ones are the most important food for polar bears.

The bearded seal is common in the whole archipelago in summer, particular in shallow waters. You are sure to find it north of Spitsbergen and Nordaustlandet, in Storfjorden and in the fjords on western Spitsbergen. It is hunted and used as food for sled-dogs.

The ringed seal is the most common species and it stays all year. You see it everywhere in sheltered fjords. It is also hunted to feed sled-dogs.

Whales

If you are lucky you can see whales. Before the whaling started in the 17th century there were many whales around Svalbard and in the fjords. Many species have not yet recovered from that hideous slaughter. Today mostly smaller whales are observed.

The bowhead whale was the species that was hunted the most by the whalers and is today very rare in Svalbard waters.

The narwhale is also rare but it has been seen off northwestern Spitsbergen and north Nordaustlandet. As a rule it follows the edge of the drift ice.

The pike whale is found north of Svalbard at the edge of the drift ice in summer. It also swims along the coast and enters the fjords. It is curious and swims and plays around boats, sometimes even jumps out of the water at them.

The right whale does not sink to the bottom when killed and was therefore almost exterminated in the 1600s. Today it is extremely rare.

The white whale, Beluga, is the whale you usually see. It is the most common of all whales and you spot it swimming like a white stripe at the surface of the sea along the coast and in the fjords. It frequents the estuaries of the larger fjords, for example Adventelva at Longyearbyen, but it also follows the edge of the ice or swims in the drift ice.

Seals hung to dry to be food for sled-dogs

Walrus

The walrus is found in the whole archipelago, but mostly in the eastern parts. It is a very funny animal to watch. If you avoid scaring these strange creatures you can get very close to them. They are very curious, and if you stand still on the shore or sit still in the dinghy they will come swimming to check what kind of object you may be. A walrus is a lumbering animal on land but an animal well suited to life in Arctic waters. If you approach walruses when they are asleep on the shore they are slow to wake and often look up several times before realizing that there are strangers close by. The moment they have decided to go into the water they do it accompanied by thundering splashes.

The male is three or four metres long and the female between two and three metres. The male weighs from 800 to 1500 kilos while the female weighs from 600 to 900 kilos. A young one is born in spring and weighs 60 kilos and is more than one metre long.

The walrus lives in flocks and enjoys staying on ice floes. When these have melted they prefer a gravel or pebbled shore. But they want to be close to the sea. They are lumbering on the shore and find it difficult to get down into the water. They go to a great deal of trouble trying to crawl or roll around sideways to dive in.

Walruses live on shell-fish that they find thanks to their effective but very sensitive whiskers. They also feed on other animals of the sea bottom and catch fish.

Birds

About 160 different bird species have been seen on Svalbard, but only 25 of them breed there every year and migrate in winter to the Norwegian Sea, the North Sea and the European coast on the Atlantic. Most birds live close to the sea. Many fly hours and hours over the sea, looking for food. There are fifteen bird reserves along the western coast of Spitsbergen. There are many bird rocks with tens of thousands, even hundreds of thousands of birds of the same species. They make a terrifying noise and fly around, perch on a cliff for a moment and then rapidly take wing again.

It may seem strange that Svalbard so far north is home to so many birds.

Black guillemot

Thousands of gulls in a ravine at Diskobukta

The reason is the ocean, so rich in nutricious microorganisms could not be more favourable than here, where the icy Arctic currents meet the warm Gulf Stream. Then drift ice offers opportunities for birds to rest now and then while looking for food.

Birds regularly breeding on Svalbard:

Arctic Skua
Arctic Tern
Barnacle Goose
Black Guillemot
Brent Goose
Brünnich´s Guillemot
Eider
Fulmar
Glaucous Gull
Grey Phalarope
Ivory Gull
King Eider
Kittiwake
Little Auk
Long-tailed Duck
Long-tailed Skua
Pink-footed Goose
Ptarmigan
Puffin
Purple Sandpiper
Red-throated Diver
Ross´s Gull
Snow Bunting
Turnstone

ic tern   Red-throated diver   Ivory gull   Kittiwake

Little auk

81

Environmental Protection

The remains of Pike´s house at Danskø

The Svalbard Environmental Protection Act regulates both the protection of the environment and the protection of cultural remains. On Svalbard a general rule says that you must not leave any traces of your visit, you must not harm nature or cultural remains and you must not throw away litter or refuse.

The Arctic climate renders the thin layer of vegetation extremely vulnerable and fragile. It must not be hurt, because regrowth is a slow process - if at all possible.

All animals on Svalbard are protected except during hunting seasons. There are national parks, nature reserves, bird reserves and geotope protected areas.

Rules in all protected areas:
The following is strictly prohibited
- dumping waste
- hunting or disturbing birds or mammals
- removing plants or fossils
- driving off-road vehicles
- landing with aircraft
- erecting new buildings
- trapping activities

National Parks

Forlandet national park, 640 sq.km, is the smallest of the parks. It is the breeding site of geese and eiders and it has the world´s northernmost flock of harbour seals.

Nordenskiöld Land national park covers 1182 sq.km. Svalbard´s largest uninterrupted areas of rich vegetation are found here. In Reindalen there are extensive wetland areas that are important bird areas. In the south-western part you find large seabird colonies in Ingeborgfjellet.

North-West Spitsbergen national park covers 3.560 sq.km. Here you find huge bird colonies of sea-birds and large herds of reindeer and walruses. There are also cultural remains from the whaling of the 17th century, for instance Smeerenburg and the graveyards from many centuries. On Danskøya you find the remains of the first attempts to reach the North Pole both in a balloon and in an airship.

Northern Isfjorden national park covers 2050 sq.km. and has extensive areas with rich vegetation consisting of a variety of species. The large flat coastal areas are important biotopes for wading birds, gees and ducks.

Sassen-Bünsow Land national park, 1157 sq.km., has extensive vegetation-covered areas and wetlands which are important bird biotopes as well as seabird colonies. In Tempelfjorden you can find ringed seal.

South Spitsbergen national park covers 5.300 sq.km., and 65% of it is covered by glaciers. The bird life is rich. Among other species eiders and barnacle geese breed here.

Nature Reserves

The nature reserves are created to protect untouched or almost untouched areas. They guarantee that the ecological processes will go on, undisturbed by human activity. These areas have a great value of their own and are important reference regions for scientists. The regulations concerning Nature Reserves are stricter than those of National Parks.

Moffen nature reserve was established to protect the important breeding sites for birds and resting places for walruses.

North-East Svalbard nature reserve is the largest of the reserves, covering 19.030 sq.km. Here you meet the magnificent landscape of high Arctic Svalbard. There are numerous reindeer, seals, whales and polar bears

A stove and remains of a house in Ny London

At Danskøya there are remains from the production of hydrogen gas used in balloons and airships

living here. It is also an important breeding locality for seabirds and geese.

Ossian Sars, 11 sq.km., east of Kongsfjorden, has rich vegetation with several rare plant species. Camping is not allowed here.

South-East Svalbard nature reserve, 6.380 sq.km., covers Barentsøya, Edgeøya and Tusenøyane. There is a large population of Svalbard reindeer in the area. Walruses, whales and polar bears are also found in great numbers. In the reserve there are important breeding sites for birds.

Bird Reserves

All the 15 bird reserves lie on skerries and islands along the west coast of Spitsbergen. They have been established to protect the most important nesting and breeding grounds of brent geese, eiders and barnacle geese. All access to the bird reserves is prohibited from the 15th of May to the 15th of August. This includes traffic both on land and at sea within a 300 m zone from land or skerry.

Festningen geotope protected area

at Grønfjorden, covers 14 sq.km. In the famous Festningen profile a geological succession can be seen which was deposited over several hundred million years (Carboniferous/Tertiary). Fossil tracks of dinosaurs can also be seen here.

This skyline of peaks met the Dutch sailors when they came to the archipelago. They named it Spitsbergen, "the sharp mountains".

History

Discovery

The first mention of Svalbard occurs in an Icelandic saga from 1194; "Svalbardi fundin", Svalbard is found. In the Icelandic Landnám Book of 1230 there is a comment about sailing to Svalbard. From Langanes on north-east Iceland you need four days to sail to Svalbard, the reference states. Later attempts have proved it to be true; thanks to the Gulf Stream and favourable winds it is indeed possible to sail to Svalbard that fast.

Knowledge like this was forgotten, but in 1594 Willem Barents read the old sagas and the statement about sailing to Svalbard. He grew very interested. Years before he had sailed in Arctic waters without finding this archipelago. In May 1596 Dutch ships sailed north to try to find the North-East Passage to the Pacific.

First they reached Bjørnøya and named it after a polar bear they had found and slaughtered on the island. Then the ships continued northwards along the ice edge and discovered the north-west part of Spitsbergen. They claimed it as Dutch territory and named it Spitsbergen after the pointed mountain peaks they could see from the ships. On one of the ships Willem Barents acted as a pilot, and together with the captain of the ship he decided on their return to Bjørnøya to sail north-east in order to reach Novaya Zemlya from the north and that way find the North-East Passage. The other ships returned to Holland. North of Novaya Zemlya Barents´ ship was caught in the ice and sank, but the crew managed to reach the shore and remained there all winter. Next summer the survivors rowed south to reach the Kola peninsula. Barents died of scurvy during this voyage to Russia. At sea the survivors were discovered by the crew of a Dutch ship. Having spent the winter in Holland they had returned to the Arctic region, looking for the lost ship and its crew. Twelve men were saved

Smeerenburg. Remains of blubber stoves.

and returned to Holland.

Whaling in the 17th century

At first the Dutch were not really interested in the new land so far north. On the other hand the English got more involved, because when sailing around Spitsbergen and into the fjords

Edgeøya. Bones after massive slaughters of walruses fill the shore at Andréetangen.

they had realized the potential of whaling and walrus hunting.

Both the Dutch government and the English King gave an English company a monopoly on hunting off the coast of Spitsbergen. In the beginning walruses were hunted but due to the huge amount of whales the hunters concentrated on whaling. Every single whale rendered so much more, and that is why whaling was much more profitable in spite of all the risks involved. When the Dutch realized the possibilities of massive whale hunting and high profits they returned to the archipelago to hunt in spite of the English monopoly. They were chased away by the English, but some of the ships were allowed to stay if half of their catches were handed over to the English company. For some years the Dutch and the English took turns being masters of the region. Then there was an agreement that gave the north and south parts of the west coast to the Dutch and the region inbetween to the English. Neither the English nor the Dutch sailors knew how to kill whales so Basque whalers were contracted. At this time the Basque whalers were the only ones who knew how to whale. For hundreds of years they had hunted whales in the Bay of Biscaya. But when hunters from the other nations had learnt the skill their importance was lessened.

In 1617 the Dutch established a whaling station on Amsterdamøya at the north-west tip of Spitsbergen. At first every ship sailed to this place where there was a blubber stove, and the men boiled the blubber in big copper pots they had stored on their ships. Initially the workers lived in tents, pitched on the beach close to the stoves. Later on a whole settlement was constructed with dwelling-houses and fixed blubber stoves for large copper pots. At the peak of activity there were seven double stoves and one single used simultaneously. The copper pots could be large, often two or three metres in diameter. The buildings were both dwelling-houses, ware-houses and workshops for craftsmen at the same time. At its most there were sixteen, maybe seventeen houses on the shore, and appr. 200 persons were busy there in summer. The remains of the stoves are still there for everybody to see together with rests of houses. Archeological excavations have resulted in a fairly good picture of this settlement in the early part of the 17th

1670. The station existed as a harbour of refuge for a while, but in 1690 most of the constructions were dismantled and taken away.

Whale and Walrus hunting

Whale hunting was a very dangerous activity. Spears were used, thrown at the whales at close range. The hunters sat in small rowingboats close to the whale and had to get the spear properly caught in the whale. Having been speared the whale often reacted with desperate movements and dived down. The lines connected to the spear now had to run easily and free. If the line got caught

Ækongen. Reconstruction of a whale carcase.

century. The Dutch called their whaling station Smeerenburg, "Blubber village".

At Danskøya across the bay and in many other places there are remains of blubber stoves. Hunting was a massive and profitable operation. In the 1600s the Dutch alone engaged 150 to 250 ships and annually killed between 750 and 1250 whales. From 1612 to 1720 the Dutch alone took 60.000 whales.

In the middle of the 17th century whales grew less numerous, and Smeerenburg was abandoned about

in anything the boat risked to be thrown over, and the hunters landed in the water. Very few knew how to swim, and often hunters drowned.

Having been speared and bled to death the whale sank to the bottom of the sea. That is why it was so important to follow the injured whale and take care of it before it disappeared into the deep. Only *the right whale* floated when dead. This was the "right" whale according to the English hunters. The bowhead whale which existed in great numbers, was also hunted and

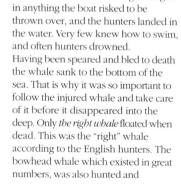

ultimately almost eradicated. The bowhead whale is a slow swimmer when moving in fjords and along the coast and obviously an easy target. The blubber was boiled to whale-oil, an important product in those days. It was used as an ingredient in the soap-industry and also as lamp-oil, in rope-production and as a binding ingredient when mixing paints. The baleens of the large whales were used as slivers in ladies' corsets.

The walrus is a fairly big animal. A male can weigh more than a 1000 kilos and a female half as much. But in spite of its size and clumsy body it is a very capable swimmer. It is very difficult to hunt in water, and there is always the risk that a male walrus will attack the rowing-boat approaching. There are stories about males hacking their tusks right through the bottom of a rowing-boat, sinking it. On shore the walrus is very lumbering and has great problems moving about. The walruses were not hunted, they were slaughtered. Hunters could walk along the shore, clubbing a herd of walruses before they managed to reach the sea. One method used was to start killing the walruses resting close to the water. The other walruses on the shore were stopped by their dead from reaching the sea, and the hunters could move on, slaughtering them as well.

On land a walrus is an easy prey

In many places along the coasts of the archipelago there are lots of bones of walruses and whales. Where skeletal remains are left nutritive substances fertilize the ground. This explains the rich vegetation close to skeletal remains even if the surroundings are bare.

The Russian Period of hunting in the 18th century

At the beginning of the 18th century the Russians started hunting walruses, seals, polar bears, Arctic foxes and birds on Spitsbergen and the other islands. The Russians were called Pomors and lived on the White Sea and Lake Onega in northwestern Russia, hunting, setting traps and fishing along the coasts. They also traded in northern Norway. Their boats were light, and using the oars the Pomors were able to manoeuvre in shallow waters and in drift ice. It is possible they had sled-dogs.

They hunted walruses on land or on the ice using spears or lances. At sea they used harpoons. To kill a white whale they used nets to force the whale closer to the shore. Arctic foxes and polar bears were caught in traps, but the Pomors also used a self-releasing contraption of bow and arrow. Ptarmigans were caught in snares, made of horsehair. Eventually the Pomors built hunting posts all over the archipelago. These posts could be subdivided into smaller huts for the summer hunt. The Russian period lasted well into the 19th century. In many places on the coasts you can still see remains of Russian hunting posts. To protect themselves against evil demons and to ensure good hunting the Pomors raised big wooden crosses, so called Russian crosses. These crosses have two transverse boards at the top and one diagonal board lower down. They were raised on mounds and at points to facilitate navigation.

The Norwegian Period of hunting in the 19th century

At the end of the 18th century Norwegian traders tried to establish hunting posts in Spitsbergen, but there was no real public interest in spite of the rich booty caught. In the 1820s

however Norwegian hunters and trappers started to settle on Spitsbergen. In the beginning the Norwegians followed the Russian example and favoured large stations but later on they abandoned this. Instead the Norwegian hunters and trappers stayed far from one another in small huts and cabins and hunted alone or in very small groups. Many Norwegian hunters´ cabins are still left and can be used as temporary shelters when staying the night even today.

It was a hard life for those who decided to stay the winter, but the profits were considerable. The main booty was walruses, whose hides were used as driving belts in European industries. Other preys were Arctic foxes,

A fox trap. When the fox tried to snatch the bait under the trap it fell down onto the fox, and the weight of the stones captured the fox.

seals and reindeer. The polar bear was not hunted that much because the hunters and trappers did not have suitable weapons. Later they learnt to set up so called cocked gun-boxes. When a polar bear placed its head inside the box to take the bait, a lethal shot was released.

Scurvy

Hunters that stayed the winter on Svalbard faced great problems coping with the cold and the lack of food. Extreme difficulties met those who had had to abandon a boat caught in the ice or a boat pressed down under the ice. Often they were not properly equipped to stay the winter on Svalbard, and they lacked both suitable clothes and hunting weapons. But there are many stories about sailors who survived several winters and hardship thanks to their ingenuity. Many years could pass before they were saved and could be brought back home on a ship.

Even the hunters and trappers who stayed the winter voluntarily found it difficult, but they were usually more familiar with the Arctic climate.

Scurvy was an other danger to people in the archipelago. The symptoms of scurvy are bleeding gums, loss of teeth, dark spots on the body, swollen knees, discoloured urine, fatigue and irritating, hurting wounds. This disease also tormented all sailors during long voyages and is caused by a lack of vitamin C. The hunters picked the scurvy herb, Cochlearia officinalis, found on the shores and ate it raw or boiled. Raw meat could also help them avoid this frightening disease.

Minerals, Oil and Gas from 1860 to present times

For more than a century people have tried to make a profit out of mining on Svalbard. In particular the west coast of Spitsbergen and the fjords have tempting mineral deposits. But the climate is harsh and the

Marble mining was the reason for the settlement of Ny London

transports to trading centres long, so all attempts have failed. Only coal mining remains, and it is carried on by Norwegian and Russian companies.

The Swedish explorer A.E. Nordenskiöld formed a company together with other partners to mine phosphates at Kapp Thordsen. After renewed examinations of the find the company gave up the idea of mining it. But apart from the huts of the hunters

and trappers the oldest building left on Svalbard was built by this company at Kapp Thordsen on Isfjorden. The house is called Svenskehuset (the Swedish House) and has been used by scientists on several occasions. It is maintained by the Norwegian state. On Sassenfjorden a Swedish company tried to mine gypsum, but the find was not profitable and the mining stopped. Later on other companies have tried to make it profitable but failed. At the mouth of Van Mijenfjorden people tried to mine zinc in the 1920s but did not succeed.

On Blomstrandhalvøya in Kongsfjorden the Englishman Ernest Mansfield found marble at the beginning of the 20th century. He persuaded an English company to invest a lot of money in shipping constructions for marble-mining to the place. He called his settlement Ny London. Remains of a harbour and a narrow-gauge railroad as well as lifting cranes are still there to see today.

Higher up on the hill-side there are characteristic buildings left. Four houses of this type were moved to Ny-Ålesund to be used there.

In addition to this there are remains of workshops, a boiler, a steam-engine, driving wheels, lifting cranes etc. Here work went on between 1910 and 1920 with the exception of the First World War. A few test minings were made, and some marble was sent to England. When the marble was lifted off the ship, it had broken into tiny pieces, probably because of slight fissures, formed in the deposit itself in the faults at Kongsfjorden millions of years ago. The deposit has been reexamined, but the quality is not good, and no further mining has been attempted.

As early as 1918 a small gas find was discovered at Grønfjorden. Since the beginning of the 1960s companies have drilled for oil and gas at Spitsbergen, Edgeøya and Hopen. No profitable finds have been made so far. Nobody knows if there are oil deposits on or off Svalbard. Svalbard is a protrusion of the continental shelf and can be regarded as a continuation from the North Sea and the Norwegian Sea, but the latest explorations give no indications of oil or gas in the region. This is greeted with joy by all who want to protect the unique nature of Svalbard. People worry about the damages possible oil industries could cause. There is a risk of a conflict between economical and ecological interests if the oil companies would concentrate on exploring the Svalbard region.

The lifting crane was used when mining marble

Coal mining from 1900 to the present

The coal on Spitsbergen was formed during the Carboniferous, Jurassic and Tertiary periods. The most impressive layers date from the Tertiary period (60 - 70 millions of years ago). They can be several metres broad. Most of the coal already mined was taken out of streams of 60 - 80 centimetres´ breadth. The coal is dense and shiny and has a high heating quality and a very low proportion of ashes and humidity. It is found at Isfjorden and in the areas southwards towards Van Mijenfjorden. There are also streams of coal at Kongsfjorden, but mining has stopped there. The coal of Spitsbergen has been classified as suitable for use in metallurgic processing.

When mining you enter the edge of the mountain where the seams are formed, and then you work farther into the mountain along the seam. At Longyearbyen there are several places where you can see entrances like this on the mountain slopes.

In the 17th century even the whalers knew there was coal on Svalbard, but nobody in England or Holland was interested in the mining prospects. The cold winter conditions including ice and transport difficulties worked against the idea of mining on Svalbard. In the latter part of the 19th century geological surveys were made by Swedish scientists like Otto Torell, A.E. Nordenskiöld, Gustaf Nordenskiöld,

60 cu.m. of coal from the find at Isfjorden. Together with three other Norwegians he had formed a company for coal-mining. But they had many problems getting banks and undertakers interested. The man who started serious coal mining on Svalbard was the American industrialist John Munro Longyear. He had bought iron-ore mines in northern Norway and saw a possibility of shipping coal from Svalbard to use in the refining of the iron-ore. In 1906 he founded the Arctic Coal Company and immediately began exploratory mining at Adventfjorden. At the same time all the different buildings and constructions were built, everything needed for a community with coal miners, employees and all necessary services. A harbour and an elevated cableway were also set up. After a few years, mining was well under way, but the First World War made it difficult to find skilled workers. In 1916 Longyear sold his company to the Norwegian company Store Norske Spitsbergen Kulkompani, usually called Store Norske. Today the company is

Longyearbyen. The white building is the Svalbard Museum. You can see the entrance of the American Mine, on the mountain slope straight above the museum.

A.G. Nathorst and Gerard de Geer. Their results showed rich deposits of coal on Spitsbergen. In the summer of 1899 the Norwegian captain Søren Zachariassen arrived at Tromsø with owned by the Norwegian State. Coal is mined at Adventdalen just outside Longyearbyen and in Sveagruva at Van Mijenfjorden.

Sveagruva is a mine that was opened by Swedish shareholders in 1916. In 1934 the mine was sold to Store Norske Spitsbergen Kulkompani. To get skilled workers men were recruited from the coal mines in southern Sweden, where similiar techniques were used.

Not only Swedish and Norwegian companies were engaged in coalmining. Both Dutch and Russian companies showed a marked interest in the deposits. The Dutch started mining at Grønfjorden and founded a mining community they called Barentsburg. In 1932 the Russians bought the entire area with buildings and constructions. Since then they have mined coal there. Earlier the Russians had taken over the coal mining at Pyramiden at Billefjorden. It was started by a Swedish company. The Russian coal company had also tried mining coal at Grumant between Longyearbyen and Barentsburg.

Longyearbyen. A statue of a miner. Often the coal seams were 60 to 80 cm wide.

The coal-mining operated by Store Norske close to Longyearbyen will eventually be closed down. Instead all extraction will be concentrated to Sveagruva and other areas where there are very rich deposits of coal, for instance in the region between Isfjorden and Van Mijenfjorden.

Remains of coal-mining equipment can be seen in many places. At Longyearbyen there are both the entrances to the mines on the slopes of the mountains and the remains of the elevated cableways from the mines. You can not avoid seeing the almost spider-like building on the north side of the valley at the industries and the harbour. This is Taubanesentralen, the cableway centre where all cableways met and from where the coal was taken by cableway to the coal harbour to be loaded on ships and exported. Farther down the slope there is a cableway switch for two of the cableways. At the museum you can see an engine and some coal cars used inside the mine.

At Ny-Ålesund coal was mined by another Norwegian company, but the mine was closed in 1962 after a severe mine accident. Today parts of the earlier railroad and a locomotive with some coal cars are shown in the harbour. It is a nice photo opportunity! This is the northernmost train.

Tourism from the 1890s to present times

Today tourism is an important part of Svalbard´s commercial and industrial life. As early as the end of the 19th century Norwegian, English and German travel agencies tried to arrange cruises to Svalbard. In 1897 the first hotel was opened at the hotel-isthmus on the mouth of Adventfjorden. The guests could take part in wildlife walking tours, boat excursions in Isfjorden and reindeer hunting. There were also opportunities to go to Danskøya by boat and see the balloon-house Andrée built. Some of the visitors were also able to meet the members of his expedition before they left in the balloon for the North Pole.

These tourist cruises continued during

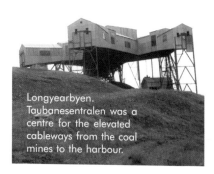

Longyearbyen. Taubanesentralen was a centre for the elevated cableways from the coal mines to the harbour.

Nordpol Hotellet was opened three days after the outbreak of the Second World War in 1939. It was closed straight away and opened after the end of the war.

the first part of the 20th century. In the 1930s "hurtigrutten", a line of Norwegian coastal steamers, left Hammerfest for Svalbard for the first time. There were five tours every summer. After the Second World War this traffic was resumed, only to be stopped in the beginning of the 1980s. Airlines now took over. But some shipping companies still traffic the west and north-west coast of Spitsbergen every summer. At some very interesting places along the coast passengers are taken in rubber boats to the shores. Boat traffic is very lively in summer in the archipelago. Ice conditions permitting, many of the smaller ships tour the whole group of

islands and let their passengers come ashore.

The present airport at Longyearbyen was built in 1974 and airlines today bring thousands of tourists to and from Svalbard. The number of tourists has increased every year. In 1990 appr. 34.000 people came by air, and that number was doubled in ten years time. Almost 1000 tons of goods are freighted by air, a part of it fresh goods like milk and vegetables and 400-500 take-offs of regular flights or package tours are registered.

Travelling is an all-year-phenomena, but most tourists visit Svalbard in summer. There is comparatively much winter tourism based on adventure activities. Norwegian companies, authorities and organizations arrange courses and conferences at Longyearbyen in autumn, winter and spring. All this provides a resonable basis for hotels at Longyearbyen.

Within Svalbard a number of helicopter flights for tourists are arranged, mostly to Ny-Ålesund. Sysselmannen´s air inspections are numerous and important, and so are the transports of patients by air. The airport at Longyearbyen shows a total of more than 2.000 take-offs per year.

Research Before 1950

Having discovered Spitsbergen in 1596 the Dutch sailed to this northern archipelago several times, and maps were drawn of the region. During the latter part of the 19th century a systematic mapping of all Svalbard was begun. Swedes, Russians and Norwegians were employed, and the work was completed at the beginning of the 20th century.

The German F. Martens went to Spitsbergen in late 1600s and studied plants and birds.

The famous Swedish biologist Carolus Linnæus, who lived in the 18th century, sent one of his students, A.R. Martin on a voyage to Spitsbergen and east Greenland.

In 1773 the Englishman Phipps made the first scientific research on geography. He was in 1827 followed by W.E. Parry, from England too, who made geological investigations and signed maps. In the same year the

Ny-Ålesund. The camp site is situated on the other side of the river and its lavatory right in the middle over the river.

Norwegian B.M. Keilhau studied geology and botany.

The Swedish scientist Sven L. Lovén travelled to Spitsbergen in 1837 to explore marine life in Arctic waters. In 1858 Otto Torell continued this work, but he also looked at other material, for instance fossils. Nordenskiöld was a member of this exploration team, and during the following years he made several voyages to Svalbard. He spent the winter of 1872/73 together with other scientists at Mosselbukta on the northern part of Spitsbergen.

In 1882/83 Swedish scientists took part in the First Geophysical Year and stayed the winter at Svenskehuset at Kapp Thordsen. The leader of the group was Nils Ekholm and one of the participants was S.A. Andrée who tried to reach the North Pole in a balloon in the 1890s.

After 1950

During the last decades many countries have located their research to Svalbard. There are scientific research stations in all the three communities of Longyearbyen, Ny-Ålesund and Barentsburg. At Ny-Ålesund several countries now house their scientists in buildings of their own. At Longyearbyen there is UNIS, a branch of the Norwegian universities. Research is carried on and academic studies on various levels offerred. Norway has also transferred parts of its work within Norsk Polarinstitutt to Svalbard.

Apart from education UNIS is engaged in several projects in Arctic science. Most teachers and researchers come from Norway, but there are a number of lecturers and researchers from other European countries. At UNIS there are about 25 teachers and scientists and 15 technicians and administrators.

University Education

UNIS is the short for "The University Courses on Svalbard", and it is a branch of the four Norwegian universities in Oslo, Bergen, Trondheim and Tromsø. They get government grants to carry out scientific research on Svalbard. You can see this activity as a part of the Norwegian scientific exploration of Arctic areas close to the North and the South Pole.

UNIS was founded in 1993, and already in 1995 the first university building was ready. Its striking architecture can be understood as a reflection of the Arctic landscape it is set in.

Different courses are offered to hundreds of students. Most students live in Nybyen in modernized apartments, formerly occupied by miners. There are courses and projects in Arctic biology, Arctic geophysics and Arctic technology.

The distance between Nybyen and UNIS is three kilometres, and it is practical to have a bike when a student. Every student must learn how to drive a snow-mobile and how to use firearms if he or she runs into a polar bear. For the students who take part in fjord or sea projects there are strict rescue drills, organized by the Coast

Guards. The security of the students has top priority.

Projects of different types are supervised by researchers from 20 nations. Most researchers come from Norway. At Ny-Ålesund many countries have their own scientific posts.

Scientific research of today concerns geology, glaciology, metereology, astrophysics, biology, archeology, Arctic medicine, environment and ice-conditions at sea.

The UNIS-building in Longyearbyen

Population

Barentsburg

This Russian mining community has 800-900 Russian and Ukrainian inhabitants. Their aim is to be self-sufficient, and meat and vegetables are produced within the community. The contacts with Russia are not as frequent as those of the Norwegians with Norway.

Mining is the predominant industry. There is a textile factory where some women work. Women are also employed in the service sector. There is a museum with exhibits on geology and coal-mining, a library and a big sports hall for many different sports. Earlier there were 900 Russians at the settlement Pyramiden, but that mine is now abandoned after a fire.

Hornsund

For many years Poland has had a research station on the north side of the inflow to Hornsund on southern Spitsbergen. About 10 scientists stay there all year, and in summer they are joined by more researchers.

Ny-Ålesund

This small community is the northernmost community of the world. Here you find between 40 and 150 inhabitants depending on the season. There is a year-round population of about 40 but in summer as many as 100 join them, because many countries have their own scientific posts here.

Between 1917 and 1929 coal was mined. After the Second World War coal was extracted between 1945 and 1962, but in 1962 there was a very serious accident

Hornsund

and the mine was closed. The entire community is owned and run by the former mining company Kings Bay AS.

The scenery around Ny-Ålesund is breath-takingly beautiful, and it is easy to reach the coasts of the north-west and north part of Spitsbergen. More than a hundred years ago this region was visited by tourists.

Sveagruva

There is not a settlement at Sveagruva. The team of 250 workers stay in barracks during their working periods and are then flown to Longyearbyen when relieved by a new team.

Longyearbyen

Longyearbyen is named after the American industrialist and mine owner John Munro Longyear. In 1906 he began extracting coal in Adventdalen. The community has been totally dependent on coal-mining until the last decades. Today tourism, Arctic science and coal-mining are the three main assets of the community. Within some years mining in Adventdalen will cease and be replaced by more intense mining at Sveagruva.

During the Second World War all communities, settlements and mines were bombed and burnt down by German forces. Immediately after the war rebuilding started. The community of today is modern with all necessary facilities. There are hotels and restaurants, and in the shops you will find everything needed both by the inhabitants and the tourists. Several tour operators arrange both one-day trips and longer tours.

In Longyearbyen about 1800 persons live all year. The population has increased by 30% during the last 10 years. Most people are Norwegian citizens, but there are also citizens from other Scandinavian and European countries. Longyearbyen has a young population with a high level of education. About 20% are under the age of 20, while a little more than 50% are between 20 and 45 years old. Less than 25% are older than 45, and only a few have reached retirement.

During the summer season the population increases because of seasonal workers. There is some lack of housing for the year-round population. Every year new blocks of flats are built. Some people return to Norway every year and new people arrive. It is usual to sign a contract to work on Svalbard for a certain period of time, often two or three years. The contract can be prolonged. Some people like living on Svalbard and stay for many years. Some came to Svalbard as children with their parents and regard themselves as Svalbardians. A few retired persons stay on, in spite of the fact that the government do not want old people on Svalbard.

Almost 1200 persons are employed in various professions. The apportionment between different professions looks like this:

Profession	Percentage
Mining industry	20%
Hotels, restaurants	13%
Public employees, administration	11%
Building and construction	11%
Trade	11%
Education, Health, Social services	10%
Transport	8%
Miscellaneous	16%

At Longyearbyen there are inbetween 70 and 80 different associations and clubs, and it is common to be a member of more than one. There are associations and societies for every imaginable taste and interest. The sports hall close to the school is used for practising football, handball, floorball, volleyball, badminton, aerobics, climbing and children´s activities. You are sure to find

"No Scooter driving today!"

about 1500 snowmobiles at Longyearbyen, and when there is enough snow snowmobiling is a favourite sport.

There is a well-equipped hospital in the centre with doctors, dentists, nurses and administrative staff. All in all 20 people work at the hospital. You also find an ambulance car and crew. They help people hurt in the mines and other casualties, but tourists may need medical attention too. Owing to the close contacts with the mainland people catch the same colds, flus and other diseases as in Norway. In one year the hospital is visited by about one thousand patients, and about one hundred patients are admitted into hospital care. Some patients are flown to Norway straight away for specialist treatment. Appr. 100 flight transports take place every year. The church employs a minister and an assistant. While the assistant mainly works with children and teenagers the minister shall serve all inhabitants of Svalbard, regardless of religion and belief. He can ask for assistance from Norway and arrange for Catholic priests to visit the Polish scientists at Hornsund and Orthodox popes to hold Mass at Barentsburg.

Wages and salaries are higher than on the mainland. Civil servants for example have the same level of salaries as in

Norway plus an extra Svalbard addition. Rents vary; some have free housing, heating and electricity while others pay between 8.000 and 10.000 NKr per month for a bigger apartment. Some companies have their own houses and can offer lower rents. Apart from the cost of housing the actual cost of living in Svalbard is lower than in Norway. Prices have gone up during the last years and now almost reach the level of prices in Norway. Many try to find work on Svalbard because it is thought to be

Dwelling-houses in Longyearbyen

The church in Longyearbyen

quite profitable to work there for a couple of years. Usually there are many applicants to single job. The income tax in Svalbard is appr. 15%, much lower than in the rest of Norway. But taxes on property are the same as on the mainland.

Shops in Longyearbyen offer everything from groceries to sport equipment. Prices are lower than on the mainland but tend to rise. Food is fairly expensive, in particular fresh goods like fruit, vegetables, eggs and dairy products. Even clothing costs more than on the mainland. Svalbard is a tax-free-zone, and this explains the cost levels and particularly the pricing of wine, beer and spirits. You pay only half of what is asked on the mainland. It is also much cheaper to buy a car, a snowmobile and a motorbike here than in the rest of Norway, simply because there is no value-added-tax or any other fiscal taxes.

In Longyearbyen there are about 800 registered cars, and many people invest in a car for conveniency and security reasons. Meeting a polar bear on a dark winter´s day right among the houses, that is not dangerous when you are inside a car. In winter many parents take their children to and from school by car.

The school at Longyearbyen is modern and has about 200 students. 35% of them go to the lower junior level of school, 25% to the upper junior level and 20 % to the lower secondary school. 20% attend the upper secondary school and concentrate mostly on theoretical studies. Some of them prefer to go to upper secondary schools on the mainland.

UNIS, the university branch at Longyearbyen, has 25-30 employees and about 100 students plus at least 100 researchers on a year-round basis.

There is also a number of researchers at the Norsk Polarinstitutt (Norwegian Polar Institute) working the year round. In summer more scientists join them.

Svalbard becomes a Part of Norway

Ever since Svalbard was discovered at the end of the 16th century it was considered an international common ground. Anyone could go to Svalbard and hunt whales, walruses, polar bears and Arctic foxes. But at first there were some disputes between nations about the monopoly on whaling. During the 19th century many countries set up scientific posts and there was little opposition.

But coal-mining meant that very strong economic interests became involved. Laws and regulations were needed to solve conflicts between different companies and countries, but also between companies and workers. Several attempts at finding an international solution were made. What country was going to gain sovereignty and what legislation was necessary to rule the archipelago? Norway had great interests on Svalbard, and so had Russia/the Soviet Union.

In connection with the Treaty of Versailles after the First World War the Svalbard Treaty was signed in 1920 and Norway was given sole sovereignty over Svalbard from 1925. Apart from Norway 39 nations signed the Svalbard Treaty.

All activities are governed by

legislation enacted by Norwegian authorities. Norway is obliged to grant equal rights to citizens and companies from all the parties to the Treaty in

clearly defined fields:
* Entrance to and residence on
  Svalbard
* Fishing and hunting
* Maritime, industrial, mining and
  commercial activities
* Acquisition, enjoyment and exercise
  of property rights, including mineral
  rights

In these fields Norwegian authorities must ensure that, when the legislation is enacted and enforced no one is treated differently on the basis of nationality.

Svalbard is in fact a demilitarized zone even if Norway has a small military unit in Coast Guard surveillance. The Treaty states that Norway has the responsibility of preserving the natural environment of Svalbard. This can mean that environmental laws and regulations risk affecting different activities on Svalbard, for instance coal-mining and tourism.

Sysselmannen, the Governor of Svalbard, is the representative of the Norwegian government. He shall ensure compliance with the Treaty. It is important to uphold Norwegian sovereignty and make sure that citizens from all parties to the Treaty are granted equal rights.

A number of administrative services are carried out by Sysselmannen´s office. Sysselmannen is police and environmental authority, he is in charge of passport controls, he is a marriage official and the controller of all traffic on land and at sea. Environmental protection is vitally important, and Sysselmannen´s office works together with the coal companies and the local tour operators to solve occurring problems.

A very crucial task is the responsibility of rescue work on Svalbard. People can get lost or hurt themselves, but there can also be frightening oil spills. Sysselmannen has helicopters, boats, cars, cross country trucks and liason equipment at his disposal to succeed in all kinds of rescue operations.

The taxes, fees and charges collected shall benefit Svalbard only. The income tax on Svalbard is lower than on the mainland. The Norwegian state adds millions of NKr annually to pay for the responsibilities and the administration of Sysselmannen´s office.

Scientific Research on Svalbard

The discovery of Svalbard in 1596 was made by Dutch seamen looking for the northeast passage to China and India. In several books published in late 1590s and at the beginning of 1600s the discovery was described. The first maps of Svalbard were enclosed in some of this books. The Englishman Hudson went in 1607 to Spitsbergen, which was the name of the archipelago at that time, and studied the west coast of that island and found that there was a great number of whales.

As a result English whalers started hunting whales supported by Basque whalers. The English whalers were followed by whalers from many other countries, for instance Holland, Germany and Denmark. During all these hunting expeditions a lot of different discoveries were made. Maps of almost all of the archipelago were made.

One of the first scientific researches on Spitsbergen was made by the German F. Martens from Hamburg. He studied bird life and was the first scientist to collect plants. In 1675 Martens published a book in which he reported on his discoveries and gave a scientific description of the archipelago. His book was widely read and well-known.

The Swedish scientist A. R. Martin, who was a student of Carolus

W.E. Parry from England tried to reach the North Pole by sledlike boats but had to turn back at latitud 82° 43´ N. The drift ice moved southwards and he had to give up. He went also to Hinlopen and made geological

Linnæus, made a scientific expedition to Spitsbergen and the Arctic Ocean west of the island in 1758. During three months he worked with meteorologic observations and zoological investigations and reached the latitud 80° N.

The first scientific research in geography was made by the Englishman Phipps in 1773. His aim was to reach the North Pole but he came no further north than 80° 37´ N at Sjuøyane. He was the first who described the ivory gull.

In 1827 two expeditions took place.

investigations and designed maps of this area.

That same year the Norwegian B. M. Keilhau studied geology and botany on Spitsbergen.

In 1837 the Swede Sven Lovén who was a geologist and zoologist made a scientific expedition along the west coast of Spitsbergen and the fjords. He wanted to investigate the marine animal life of the Arctic Ocean. Twenty years later the Swedish scientist Otto Torell carried out an expedition to Spitsbergen and collected a lot of material. He also investigated glaciers and moraine formations.

In 1861 Torell made the first interdisciplinary expedition to an Arctic region. During his journey along the western and northern coast of Spitsbergen and the north coast of Nordaustlandet he collected material of different kinds and investigated the possibilities of mapping this part of Svalbard.

A.E. Nordenskiöld is the great Swedish scientist in Arctic research. He set out on expeditions in 1864 and 1868 and continued the mapping work and collected a lot of scientific material and fossils.

In 1872 his next expedition started with the intention of staying the winter at Mosselbukta. Nordenskiöld travelled to Sjuøyane and crossed the glacier of Nordaustlandet. The expedition studied and investigated magnetism, meteorology, air electricity, northern lights, astronomy, ground temperature, tide, geology and glaciology.

In 1882-83 a Swedish expedition stayed at Svenskehuset at Kapp Thordsen. The leader was Nils Ekholm and one of the members

Bird cliff

was S.A. Andrée, who in 1897 tried to reach the North Pole by balloon. Within this First Geophysic Year investigations were made concerning topography, air electricity, earth magnetism, meteorology, northern lights and tide.

In 1890 Gustaf Nordenskiöld led an expedition to Van Mijenfjorden and discovered the enormous coal deposit north of the fjord. Today this coal is mined at Sveagruva by the Norwegian coal company.

As mentioned S.A. Andrée in 1897 tried to reach the North Pole by balloon. He failed and the three men disappeared. By a coincidence their camp was found at Kvitøya in 1930. *Read more in the chapter Andrée's North Pole Expedition.*

During 1898-1902 Sweden and Russia cooperated in mapping Spitsbergen. The expeditions also made investigations to determine if the earth is flattened and how much in the northern region.

Danskøya

From the book THE ANDRÉE DIARIES

In 1882/83 he took part in a scientific expedition to Svalbard. Together with the other scientists he stayed the winter at Svenskehuset at Kapp Thordsen.

Andrée´s North Pole Expedition

Afterwards he was employed by the Swedish Patent and Registration Office, and he also founded a supportive society for inventors.

Samuel August Andrée was born in 1854 in the Swedish town of Gränna. He was the son of a pharmacist. Having graduated from grammar school in Jönköping he studied at the Stockholm Institute of Technology, today known as the Royal Institute of Technology. In 1876 Andrée went to the United States and worked at the Swedish Pavillion at the World Exhibition in Philadelphia. This made it possible for him to visit all the other interesting pavillions without paying. In the United States he met an American balloonist but he never found the opportunity to sail in a balloon himself.

From the book THE ANDRÉE DIARIES

He was the first Swede to buy a balloon of his own, and he experimented during many flights with different methods of steering it. In 1894 he told the polar explorer Nordenskiöld that he wanted to reach the North Pole in a balloon. Both the Swedish King Oscar II and Alfred Nobel greeted the idea with enthusiasm and donated money. A balloon was ordered at a French textile factory and a number of special equipment details were designed.

In 1896 his team was brought to Spitsbergen onboard the ship the Virgo, and at Danskøya in north-west Spitsbergen a balloon-house was built. The balloon was kept inside it, and gradually it was filled with hydrogen gas from a special construction for gas produce. The raw materials used in producing hydrogen gas were sulphuric acid, iron-filings and water. When the balloon was filled everybody waited for southerly winds. In the middle of August it was too late to start the flight to the North Pole. All activity was stopped and the team returned to Sweden. The winds had been unfavourable.

In the summer of 1897 Andrée was back on Danskøya already at the end of May, and a month later the balloon was filled. On the 11th of July there was a southerly wind and the balloon rose towards the north. Andrée named the balloon the Eagle.

The balloon was sealed by glue. In order to discover leakages white strips of cloth were placed on the balloon. Remains of sulphur in the hydrogen gas marked by black spots on the cloth where the leakages were to be found and thereby it was possible to seal the leakages.

Together with Andrée in the gondola or car under the balloon were Nils Strindberg and Knut Frænkel. Frænkel was a replacement for Nils Ekholm who had been a member of the team in 1896. He left the team because of his doubts about the opportunities for the balloon to manage to fly according to the great leakage of gas.

At first the balloon flew according to plans, but after twenty-four hours the winds changed directions, and the balloon was blown both to the west and to the east. On the 14th of July the balloon was weighed down, heavy with moisture and ice. It could not fly anymore. It collapsed on the drift ice. The three men now began walking on the ice towards the south to reach one of the places where they had stored supplies on Svalbard and Franz Josef Land. Their walk was extremely difficult; they faced cracks and lanes and endless walls of ice. And the ice moved all the time, so even if they walked south they sometimes drifted farther north. They managed to shoot polar bears and seals to add to the original provisions.

During their walk the three men fell ill, probably because of trichina poisoning. In September they decided to build an ice hut on the floe to stay the winter.

But at the beginning of October the floe broke and they had to try to find land. They happened to be just off Kvitøya, and they managed to carry their equipment onto the shore. They set up their camp on the western part of Kvitøya, today called Andréeneset.

The 5th of October is the last day mentioned in Andrée´s diary. He probably died soon after. Nils Strindberg was the first of the team to die, and he was buried in a rocky cave, his body covered with big stones. We do not

116

know how long Andrée and Frænkel survived after his death. They were exhausted. Their equipment was not suited for staying the winter. Some of it had also been lost when the ice floe with the hut broke.

For many years nobody knew what had happened to the three men. Rescue teams were sent to the east coast of Greenland, to Spitsbergen and Barents´ Sea. In 1898 one expedition went ashore on Kvitøya, but nobody noticed the camp of the balloonists.

The summer of 1930 was extremely warm, and snow and ice melted fast. By chance a Norwegian scientific expedition went ashore on Kvitøya and discovered the rests of Andrée´s camp. They assembled the finds and proceeded east to continue their intended explorations. Eventually it became known that Andrée´s expedition had been found and journalists tried to get more

information. The Swedish newspaper the Dagens Nyheter had a reporter, Knut Stubbendorff, who rented a fishing-boat, sailed to Kvitøya and found more of the camp. He also saved more of the men´s diaries. Rolls of film could partly be developed and showed the three men on the ice from the 14th of July to the end of September.

By means of new computer technique it was in 2003 possible for a Swedish researcher to discover more details of these rolls. We can now study these pictures and see how life on the ice was from the day of landing and during the walk until the end of September.

The remains of the three men were taken to Tromsø, and there was a memorial service. The Swedish warship the Svensksund, on which the men had travelled to Danskøya in 1897, brought the three coffins back to Stockholm. There they were greeted as national heroes and awarded every imaginable mark of honour.

After the funeral at the Storkyrkan (the Cathedral) the bodies were cremated. The three men are buried together in a grave at the Norra kyrkogården in Stockholm.

Strenuous ice walking

To the North Pole by Airship

In 1906-1909 the American journalist Walter Wellman made several attempts to reach the North Pole in an airship. He had Danskøya as his base and built hangar, dwelling-houses, storehouses and a construction for producing hydrogen gas.

All the attempts failed however; the airship rose and sailed for some hours in the air but never came further north than Norskøyane. After the last attempt in 1909 the airship exploded when it was on its way back to the hangar. In spite of all misfortunes Wellman was determined to make a new try next year to reach the North Pole in a new airship. But he gave up all those plans when he got the news that the American Peary had reached the North Pole across the ice.

In Ny-Ålesund there is an anchor pylon for airships. It was built for the airship the Norway in which the Norwegian Amundsen and the Italian Nobile reached the North Pole in 1926. Today the pylon is a cultural monument and can be regarded as a symbol of polar research in Ny-Ålesund.

Amundsen was the first man to reach the South Pole, which he did in 1911, and he also planned to get to the North Pole. Already in 1909 Peary had reached the North Pole and the American Byrd reported in 1926 that he had come to the North Pole by

In memory of Amundsen´s and Ellsworth´s flight in 1925. You find the memorial in Ny-Ålesund.

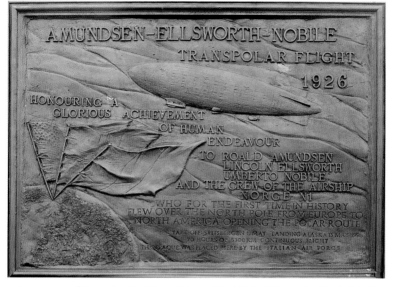

In memory of Amundsen's, Ellsworth's and Nobile's flight to the North Pole in 1926. The memorial stands near the anchor pylon in Ny-Ålesund.

airplane.

Both of these polar trips have been questioned. An investigation in 1989 stated that Peary's report was true and he is now regarded as the first man on the North Pole. Byrd's report about his flight to the pole has been checked and it is today decided that he did not reach the North Pole.

In 1925 Amundsen and the American

Ellsworth started in two airplanes from Ny-Ålesund towards the North Pole. They were however forced to make an emergency landing on the polar ice and one of the planes was destroyed. After facing hardships they succeeded in getting to Nordaustlandet and were later rescued.

Next year Amundsen, Ellsworth and

Nobile left for the North Pole in the airship the Norway. Nobile had constructed the airship and was responsible for all technical details during the trip.

The North Pole was reached on 12 May and the airship went on to Point Barrow in Alaska. One of the aims of the journey was to explore the area between Canada and the North Pole. On the return the airship passed the North Pole again and was anchored in Ny-Ålesund. The expedition got known all over the world and the members were regarded as heroes.

Nobile planned to start a new expedition to the North Pole in the airship the Italia in 1928. The aim was to explore the whole area north of Sibiria, Europe, Greenland and Canada as far as to the North Pole. Due to bad weather he never succeeded in reaching the area north of Sibiria. Fog and stormy weather stopped two attempts to go far away to the east. On 23 May Nobile started the airship towards the North Pole and reached the Pole around midnight and circled over the area for more than two hours. Then he left the Pole to go back to Ny-Ålesund.

The flight to the Pole had taken less than 20 hours thanks to a strong tailwind. On the way back there was a headwind and fog and a lot of technical problems arose. The wind got stronger and the huge gas-filled airship swayed in the gusts. The headwind caused a higher consumption of fuel than calculated. The speed therefore had to be slowed down to reduce the fuel consumption. The fog was thick and it was difficult to determine the position. The airship leaked gas and was weighed down by damp and ice and the crew struggled to keep it away from the polar ice. But then suddenly the catastrophe occured; the airship crashed down to the polar ice. The gondola hit the ice and was severe damaged. Lots of the equipment were thrown out on the ice. Some of the men were badly hurt and broke their legs or sufferred other injuries. After more than 24 ours of hard work trying to return this trip ended in a disaster.

Nine men of the crew climbed off the gondola and began to investigate the damages and to gather the equipment that was thrown out on the ice.

Suddenly a strong wind lifted the airship with six men on board and it disappeared into the fog. These men were never seen again. There were no attempts ever made to rescue them.

The nine men on the ice were lucky to find a tent among the scattered equipment. The tent was about a three metres square but gave the possibility of some shelter against wind and rain.

The radio was found, too, and after some trouble one of the men succeeded in starting it and then sent S.O.S. and listened to calls.

As the S.O.S. signals were not heard by the outside world it was decided that three men had to walk on the ice to reach the northern islands of Svalbard and hopefully find help. Two Italians survived but the Swedish scientist Finn Malmgren died during this hard ice walk.

It was a long time before the

Towards the North Pole

From the book MÄNNEN PÅ ISFLAKET

outside world got to know what had happened. The S.O.S. signals were not heard by the Italian ship that had anchored in Kongsfjorden. It was a Russian radio amateur who first listened to the S.O.S.

Now a struggle of power arouse how to organize the rescue. The Italians meant that they were responsible for the rescue. But both the Norwegians and the Swedes also felt responsibility for rescuing the crew.

The six men on the ice struggled against all the difficulties they met: frost, fog, wind, damp and lack of food. The food rations were very small and it was an extremely tough situation.

One man died and when a polar bear began to be interested in the body it was necessary to put the dead man down into a hole in the ice. Many polar bears visited the camp and one was shot. So the men´s food rations increased.

The rescue work turned out to be difficult. The weather was very disadvantageous; strong winds and fog made it impossible for airplanes to fly more than a few hours during each rescue attempt.

Gradually different rescue work came into operation. Pilots, Italian soldiers and Norwegian hunters with dogsleds tried in different ways to reach the men on the ice. Food and equipment of different kinds were thrown down from airplanes.

Roald Amundsen left Tromsø together with six men to take part in the rescue work. But the airplane was lost between Norway and Svalbard and another rescue operation had to be launched. The plane and the men were never found.

A Swedish airplane succeeded in landing on the ice near the camp and brought Nobile back to Kongsfjorden. Nobile now was accused of saving himself first of all and leaving the crew on the ice. He was condemned by the Italian government and the world press.

The Russian icebreaker the Krassin went all the way from Leningrad to

The camp on the ice

Svalbard to take part in the rescue work. The ice situation was extremely difficult north of Svalbard and the Krassin got stuck in the ice but managed to continue. After a very hard voyage the ship succeeded in rescuing the two men who had started the walk on the ice to find help. Then the Krassin found the five men at the ice camp and brought all men back to Kongsfjorden.

The consequences of the whole story were that the Italian authorities stated that Nobile was responsible and guilty. He was stripped off his rank and was forced to leave Italy for many years. The Norwegians mourned for Amundsen, their hero, and Sweden grieved for Finn Malmgren´s death.

The Russian icebreaker the Krassin

How often is the wind velocity more than 10 m/s on Svalbard?

Every third day:	November, December, January, February, March, April
Every fourth day:	May, October
Every seventh day:	June, September
Every two weeks:	July, August

Effects of Cold – Temperature and Wind

	Temperature in sheltered places (°C)						
	0	-5	-10	-15	-20	-25	-30
Wind m/s	Urgent temperature because of effects of cold (°C)						
5	-10	-16	-23	-29	-35	-41	-48
10	-14	-20	-28	-36	-42	-49	-57
15	-17	-25	-33	-41	-48	-56	-63
20	-18	-26	-34	-42	-49	-57	-64
25	-20	-28	-36	-44	-52	-60	-67

Lower than -10°C = Risk of frost injuries.
Lower than -25°C = Great risk of injuries!
Lower than -50°C = Extreme risk of injuries!!

Explanation of Geological Terms

Ammonites are an extinct group of cuttlefish with spiral shells. They were very common in the Jurassic and Cretaceous periods, i.e. 210-65 m. years ago.

Basalt is a dark and finegrained eruptive rock that is shaped when the magma has reached the surface of the earth.

Brachiopods are mussel-like and live anchored to the sea bottom by a muscular stalk. Some species live today but they were very common from the Cambrian to the Permian period, i.e. 570-245 m. years ago.

Continental drift. The earth´s crust consists of a number of large continental plates that move in relation to one another. When they crash into each other high mountain ranges can be created for example the Alps, the Himalayas, the Appalachian Mountains and the Andes.
If the continental plates apart there will be a crack in the sea bottom and magma from the inner of the earth wells out and creates a mountain range deep in the sea. This is the case in the Atlantic where there is a mountain range from the Arctic Ocean to the Antarctic Ocean. If such a range reaches the sea surface there will be islands like Iceland, the Azores and Tristan da Cunha.

Erosion. Bedrock, boulders and stones erode by streaming water and weathering. The eroded material is transported by streaming water out to the sea and deposited on the sea bottom. After some millions of years these layers can be transformed into hard material and become different bedrocks (for instance limestone and sandstone) depending on which material it consists of. If the sea bottom raises beyond the sea level the erosion starts immediately.

Faults arise when the earth´s crust moves in different directions along a crack in the bedrock. The movements can be up-down or sideways. If the part between two faults rises there will be a horst, i.e. a "rock" ridge. If the areas outside two parallell faults rise there will be a rift valley between the two faults. On the Spitsbergen island there are many faults in the direction of NNW-SSE.

Folding of the bedrock takes place because of movements in the earth´s crust. The bedrock can be bent, folded or placed edgewise.

Frost is an irresistible rock breaker. When water fills cracks and pores in rocks and then freezes it expands ten per cents of its volume and exerts a bursting pressure of about 2000 lb. to the square inch. The rocks are ruptured and fragments are wedged apart to become loose when thaw sets in.

Geological time scale of the earth (in m. years)

Quaternary	0-2	Carboniferous	290-360
Tertiary	2-65	Devonian	360-410
Cretaceous	65-145	Silurian	410-440
Jurassic	145-210	Ordovician	440-510
Triassic	210-245	Cambrian	510-570
Permian	245-290	Precambrian	570-

Polygon ground. Areas with circles, ridges or squares of stones. The diameter can vary from some decimeters to some metres. They are created in regions with permafrost because of repeated freezing and thawing in watery ground.

Screes. Frost-shivered blocks, stones and gravel from rocks fall to lower levels on mountain slopes and accumulate there. The angle of the stone-slope is usually about 30° and can never be more than 45°.

Shoreline, raised beach and beach berm. Shoreline is the boundary between the land and the sea or the land and the lake. An older shoreline may be seen as a raised beach or a beach berm situated lower or higher than the shoreline of today.
Raised beach consists usually of gravel and stones that is deposited on the shore by the waves.
Beach berm has been formed by the erosion and deposition of gravel and stones.

Trilobites were very common in the Ordovician and Cambrian periods, i.e. 440-570 m. years ago. They belong to the same group of animals as scorpions and lived on the sea bottom. The size varied from some millimetres to half a metre.

U-shaped valleys. By the passage of a glacier through a pre-existing river valley a mantle of rock-waste is removed, the overlapping spurs are trimmed and the floor is worn down. The valley is thus widened and deepened and is eventually remodelled into a U-shaped trough with a broad floor and steep sides.
A valley eroded by streaming water gets a V-shape.

Weathering is the process by which rocks are broken down and decomposed by the action of wind, rain and temperature changes. It is the initial stage in the process of denudation. On Svalbard the most common type is repeated freezing and thawing of water in cracks and pores. It can also be a chemical process brought about by the action of substances dissolved in rain water.

Names of Svalbard

Adventdalen. Probably after the English whaler the Adventure stationed in the Isfjorden in 1656.

Akseløya. After the Norwegian schooner the Axel Thordsen which was hired by the Nordenskiöld expedition to Spitsbergen in 1864.

Alkefjellet. The mountain with auk birds. Mentioned in the 1860s.

Amsterdamøya. After the city Amsterdam.

Andréeneset. After Salomon August Andrée who in 1897 died here together with Nils Strindberg and Knut Frænkel.

Andréetangen. After the German geographer Karl Andrée who lived in the 19th century.

Augustabukta. After Marie Louise Augusta Catharine, Princess of Sachsen-Weimar-Eisenach who lived in the 19th century.

Austfonna. Means the eastern ice-cap. Named in the 1930s.

Barentsburg. After Willem Barents.

Barentsøya. After Willem Barents.

Bellsund. After the shape of the bell-like mountain near the entrance of the bay.

Billefjorden. After the Dutch whaler Cornelius Claeszoon Bille who lived in the late 17th century.

Bjørnøya. In 1596 the crew of Barents´ expedition landed on this island and a polar bear was killed and the island was named Bjørnøya.

Blomstrandhalvøya. After the Swedish chemist and geologist Christian Wilhelm Blomstrand who lived in the 19th century.

Bockfjorden. After the German Franz-Karl von Bock born in 1876.

Burgerbukta. After the Austrian photographer Wilhelm Burger dead in 1920.

Colesbukta. After Coles Park. In the 17th century an area free from snow and therefore suitable for reindeer grazing.

Coraholmen. After Productus cora, a common fossil on this island.

Danskøya. After Danish whalers who in 1631 whaled on the west coast and also had a whaling station on this island.

Diskobukta. Probably after the English Duckes Cove that was changed to Dusko in Dutch and later to Disko.

Edgeøya. After the English businessman and whaler Thomas Edge dead in 1624.

Ekmanfjorden. After the Swedish businessman and donor Johan Oscar Ekman dead in 1907.

Engelskbukta. After an English whaling station situated here in the early 17th century.

Fair Haven. Since the 17th century regarded as a good anchoring place.

Festningsodden. Situated at the very edge of a fortresslike area. Norwegian hunters named it in the 19th century.

Forlandsundet. See Prins Karls Forland.

Ginevrabotnen. After James Lamont´s yacht the Ginevra that visited Svalbard in 1858.

Gipsvika. After the gypsumrich strata in the surrounding mountains.

Grumantbyen. Grumant is the Russian name of Svalbard in fact the Russian interpretation of the name Greenland.

Gråhuken. After the gray clay and sandstone strata in the bedrock from the Devon age.

Grønfjorden. There is no specially green colour around this fjord. It was in 1610 mentioned as "This place I named the Green-haven".

Hamburgbukta. After the city Hamburg.

Hinlopen. Probably after Thymen Jacobz Hinlopen the manager of the Dutch Noordsche Compagnie in the 17th century.

Hiorthamn. After manager Fredrik Wilhelm Louis Hiort, one of the pioneers within the Norwegian coal mining on Svalbard.

Hopen. Probably after the ship the Hopewell belonging to the English whaler Thomas Marmaduke who lived in the 17th century.

Hornsund. Mentioned in 1613 after findings of reindeer horns in the fjord.

Kapp Linné. After the Swedish botanist Carolus Linnæus who lived in the 18th century.

Kapp Thordsen. After the Norwegian schooner the Axel Thordsen which was hired by the Nordenskiöld expedition to Spitsbergen in 1864.

Kinnvika. After Kinnviken, a bay in the Swedish lake Vänern.

Kong Karls Land. After King Karl I of Würtenberg. 19th century.

Kongsfjorden. Is regarded as the most beautiful fjord on Svalbard. The name can be read in Dutch writings from the 18th century.

Kronebreen. After the close lying mountain peaks Tre kroner.

Krossfjorden. A manuscript from 1610 tells that a sailor east of the fjord raised a wooden cross on which he wrote the date of his arrival in the area.

Kvadehuken. After Quade hock which indicates that it could have been difficult to navigate ships outside the cape.

Kvitøya. The White Island. Former named Giles Land. The name changed in the late 19th century.

Liefdefjorden. Possibly after the Dutch ship de Liefde, that is the loved ship.

Lilliehöökfjorden. After the Swedish captain Gustaf Bertil Lilliehöök who lived in the 19th century.

Longyearbyen. After the American businessman and mine owner John Munro Longyear, who started coal mining here in 1906.

Luciakammen. After the Austrian duchess Lucia Pálffy whose father in 1872 went on an expedition to Svalbard and Novaya Zemlya.

Magdalenefjorden. Already in the 17th century the Basque whalers gave this fjord its name after Saint Magdalena the whalers´ patron saint.

Moffen. From the 17th century. After a Dutch disparaging name of Germans in Holland or possibly of a German crew on the Dutch ship the Moffen.

Moskushamna. On this place musk oxen were landed in 1929. In 1919-1921 the place was named Hiorthamn.

Mosselbukta. Mossel could be a wrong interpretation of Mussel or named after a Dutch skipper. Possibly a derivation from mors(ch) = marsh.

Newtontoppen. After the English mathematician and physicist Isaac Newton dead in 1727.

Nordaustlandet. The north east land. Mentioned in the 18th century.

Nordenskiöldbreen. After the Swedish polar explorer Adolf Erik Nordenskiöld.

Ny London. After the city London.

Ny-Ålesund. After the city Ålesund in Norway.

Prins Karls Forland. Named already in 1610 after Prince Charles of Wales later Charles I King of England and Ireland.

Reinsdyrflya. Mentioned already in the 17th century and means the plain where there are reindeer.

Rijpfjorden. After the Dutch Jan Cornelisz Rijp born in 1570.

Rossøya. After James Clark Ross English polar explorer dead in 1862.

Sassendalen. Uncertain origin. The name was used already in the late 17th century.

Sefströmbreen. After the Swedish chemist and geologist Nils Gabriel Sefström dead in 1845.

Sjuøyane. The Seven Islands. Mentioned already in the 18th century.

Skansbukta. After Skansen the plateau mountain northeast of the bay which looks like a fortress.

Smeerenburg. After a Dutch word for blubber or train oil.

Sofiebogen. After the Austrian woman Sophie Öttingen-Öttingen.

Solvattnet. After its round form.

Spitsbergen. After the peaked mountains along the west coast of the island. Was named by Willem Barents in 1596.

Sveagruva. Swedish coal mine 1917-1925. Sold in 1934 to the Norwegian cole company Store Norske Spitsbergen Kulkompani.

Sørkapp. The south cape of the Spitsbergen island. Mentioned already in the 17th century.

Tempelfjorden. See Templet.

Templet. A mountain cut up by "channels" with blocks and stones shaping talus on the bottom. The rock consists of sedimentary strata. The mountain looks lika a Gothic temple fallen into ruins.

Torbjørnsenfjellet After Anders Torbjørnsen, Norwegian shipowner and donor.

Trygghamna. Was already in the 17th century used as a harbour of refuge. Gives a good shelter from storms and its bottom concists of clay and is therefore a good anchorage place.

Tusenøyane. The Thousand Islands. Mentioned already in the 18th century.

Van Mijenfjorden. After Willem Van Muyden, leader of the Dutch whaling fleet 1612-1613. Nordenskiöld wrote wrongly Van Mijen.

Vibebukta. After the Norwegian explorer Anders Vibe who lived in the 19th century.

Virgohamna. After the ship the Virgo which in 1896 transported Andrée´s expedition from Sweden to Svalbard.

Wijdefjorden. Means the wide fjord and is mentioned already in the 18th century.

Åsgårdsfonna. After Åsgård of the Nordic mythology.

Literature and Maps

Adams, P. *Arctic Island Hunter*. London. 1961.

Amundsen, R. *First Crossing of the Polar Sea*. Doubleday. New York. 1928.

Andrée, S., Strindberg, N. and Fraenkel, K. *The Andrée Diaries*. Bodley Head. London. 1931.

Aslov, T. A. *A Short Story of Svalbard*. The Norwegian Polar Research Institute. 1989.

Behounek, F. *Männen på isflaket. Med Italia till Nordpolen*. Lindblads förlag. Uppsala. 1928.

Confrey, M. and Jordan, T. *Icemen. A History of the Arctic and Its Explorers*. Boxtree. London.1998.

Conway, A. *No man´s Land*. Cambridge. 1906.

Den norske LOS. Vol. 7. Norwegian Hydrographic Service and Norwegian Polar Research Institute. 1988.

Farnes, O. *The War in the Arctic*. Darf. London. 1991.

Gjorevoll, O. and Rönning, O. *Flowers of Svalbard*. Tapir. 1989.

Greve, T. *Svalbard, Norway in the Arctic*. Oslo. 1975

Hisdal, V. *Geography of Svalbard*. A short survey. Norsk Polarinstitutt. Oslo. 1976.

Hjelle, A. *Geology of Svalbard*. The Norwegian Polar Institute. 1993.

Holland, C. *Arctic. Exploration and development c. 500 b.c. to 1915. An encyklopedia*. New York and London. 1994.

Liljequist, G. H. *High Lights: a History of Swedish Polar Travels and Research*. Swedish Polar Research Secretariat. Stockholm. 1993.

Liversidge, D. *The Third Front*. Severn House Publishers. 1976.

Lundborg, E. *The Arctic Rescue— how Nobile was Saved*. Viking Press. New York. 1929.

Mathisen, T. *Svalbard in the changing Arctic*. Oslo. 1954.

Martinsson, T. *Photographic Archeology and Nils Strindberg's Photographs from the Andrée Polar Expedition 1896-1897*. Diss. University of Westminster, London. 2003.

Mehlum, F. *Birds and Animals of Svalbard*. The Norwegian Polar Research Institute. Oslo. 1990.

Mollet, W. *Robert Peary and Matthew Henson at the North Pole*. Elkhorn Press. Kentucky. 1996.

Nobile, U. *My Polar Flights*. Muller. London. 1961.

Nobile, U. *With the Italia to the North Pole*. Allen and Unwin. London. 1930.

Peary, R.E. *The North Pole*. Hodder and Stoughton. London. 1910.

Sundman, P.O. *The Flight of the Eagle*. Pantheon Books. New York. 1970.

Svalbard– a Norwegian outpost. Bergen 1950.

The Place-names of Svalbard. The Norwegian Polar Research Institute. Oslo. 1991.

de Verre Gerrit. *The Three Voyages of Willem Barents*. Amsterdam 1600. English Edition. London. 1876.

Worsley, D. *The Geological History of Svalbard*. Aga-Statoil. 1986.

Wråkberg, U. (red). *The Centennial of S. A. Andrée's North Pole Expedition*. Stockholm. 1999.

- - - -

Svalbard Reiseliv/Svalbard Tourism offers different kinds of written information, for free or for sale.

Sysselmannen produces a lot of information brochures, booklets etc.

The Norwegian Polar Institute publishes regularly publications in English.

Maps
The Norwegian Polar Institute produces maps in different scales. You can find topographical maps, geological maps, tourist maps. They are sold in Longyearbyen by the Institute, the Tourist Office, Svalbardbutikken and some other shops.

INDEX

Summer morning in Isfjorden

North west of Svalbard

Come join...

The S A Andrée Polar Expedition
1897 and
The British-Norwegian-Swedish
Antarctic Expedition 1942-52.

Welcome!
Further information: +46 390 41010/15
www.grennamuseum.se
andree@grm.se

You will find our
museum between
Gothenburg and
Stockholm, by the
lake Vättern.

GRENNA
MUSEUM

ANDRÉEXPEDITIONEN
POLARCENTER